JESUS'S RETURN

BASED ON THE FEASTS OF THE LORD

Robert Parker

Robert's Trumpet
www.RobertsTrumpet.com

Copyright 2021 by Robert Parker

Published by Robert's Trumpet LLC
Winter Garden, FL

Fourth printing

ISBN: 978–1–7368588–6–8 (paperback)
ISBN: 978–1–7368588–7–5 (e–book)
ISBN: 978–1–7368588–8–2 (PDF)

Graphic illustration book cover by Inflection Studios Design, 1469 W. Menlo Ave, Fresno, CA 93711.

All rights reserved. No part of this book may be reproduced in any means—electronic digital, mechanical, or otherwise—without permission in writing from the publisher, except by a reviewer who may quote brief passages in a review.

Unless otherwise indicated, all Scripture quotations are from The Holy Bible, English Standard Version® (ESV®), copyright © 2001 by Crossway, a publishing ministry of Good News Publishers. Used by permission. All rights reserved.

Scripture quotations taken from the (NASB®) New American Standard Bible®. Copyright © 1960, 1971, 1977, 1995, 2020 by The Lockman Foundation. Used by permission. All rights reserved. www.lockman.org.

The Apocrypha of the Old Testament, King James Version (KJV) 1611, American Bible Society (ABS), New York.

This book is written to provide eschatological insights into events, which may or may not happen in our lifetimes. It is sold with the understanding that neither the author nor publisher is engaged in rendering a professional service. If legal, medical, financial or other expert assistance is required, the services of a competent professional person should be sought.

To my loving parents

Table of Contents

Preface vii
Abbreviations..viii
Definitions x
Notes xi
Introduction 1
Chapter 1: Feasts of the Lord and Fulfilled Prophecies 7
Chapter 2: Future Fall Feast Prophecies... 13
Chapter 3: History of the Feasts of the Lord Theory 17
Chapter 4: Identify the Start of the Seventieth Week of Daniel....................... 21
Chapter 5: Determine Rapture Window Dates 25
Chapter 6: Filter #1, Two Thousand Years Are Two Days 29
Chapter 7: Filter #2, Two Witnesses Arrive on a Passover 35
Chapter 8: Filter #3, 75 Days 45
Chapter 9: This Generation 49
Chapter 10: Show a Blessing to Pregnant and Nursing Women 55
Chapter 11: Ten Days of Awe.. 59
Chapter 12: Conclusion.. 75
Index 91
Scripture Index 93
Apocrypha Index 97

List of Figures

Figure 1: Beyond Prewrath Overview Timeline 2
Figure 2: Rapture Windows Timeline 3
Figure 3: Five Rapture Positions 17
Figure 4: Rapture Windows of the Elect 20
Figure 5: Seventieth Week of Daniel 22
Figure 6: Seventieth Week of Daniel with Dates 22
Figure 7: Rapture Windows of the Elect 26
Figure 8: Rapture Window Start Dates for Tishri 1 26
Figure 9: Two Thousand–Year Return of Jesus 33
Figure 10: Two Witnesses – Checking Assumption 37
Figure 11: Two Witnesses Five-Day (W1 to W6) Timeline (Great Fit) ... 41
Figure 12: Two Witnesses Seven-Day (W1 to W8) Timeline (Poor Fit) .. 41
Figure 13: Yom Kippur to Hannukah – 75 Days 46
Figure 14: 30- and 45-Day Segments 47
Figure 15: Day 1 Dates – All in Spring and Not on a Sabbath 56
Figure 16: Ten Days of Awe 60
Figure 17: Work Days for 1,252, 1,254, and 1,255 62
Figure 18: Jehoshaphat Battle 69
Figure 19: Overview – Based on 14 May 1948 Birth 77
Figure 20: Overview – Based on 7 June 1967 Birth 77
Figure 21: Beginning of Seventieth Week of Daniel 78
Figure 22: Parallels between Matthew 24 and Revelation 6–8 81
Figure 23: Beyond Prewrath Overview Timeline 81
Figure 24: Window Dates When Great Tribulation Ends Confirmed with 24 Hour Darkness 82
Figure 25: When to Begin and End Hiding in Your Chamber 85
Figure 26: Fifth Seal to First Trumpet 86

Preface

This theory is based on the three fall feasts of the Lord having end-time prophetic meaning, just as the earlier four spring Feasts of the Lord had prophetic meaning with Jesus first coming. Several other scholars have proposed this eschatological understanding of the fall feasts of the Lord, though I am taking it to its logical conclusion of date setting.

If this author's first book *Beyond Prewrath End–Time Prophecy* was controversial, then this book with the Feasts of the Lord will be much more. The seventieth week of Daniel is expected to start on one specific 24-hour Jewish day, either 13 November 2023; 9 November 2026; or 23 October 2063. The 2023 and 2026 dates are derived from when Israel became a nation on 14 May 1948. The 2063 date is derived from when Israel took control of the temple mount on 7 June 1967.

The Feasts of the Lord theory manuscript was started May 2019, and then March 2020 it was laid aside to begin writing a separate book *Beyond Prewrath End–Time Prophecy*, which was published May 2021. It was updated May 2022.

The second and third print take the *Beyond Prewrath End-Time Prophecy* position that *little while* is considered 40 to 46 days versus an exact 40 days. This points to hiding in your chamber six days sooner (figures 25 and 26) to avoid the intense persecution (fury) near the end of the great tribulation. The fourth print provides a better description of the Jewish calendar discrepancy on page 77.

Abbreviations

The abbreviation Day 1 is used frequently for the middle of the seventieth week of Daniel. It refers to when the abomination of destruction of the temple occurs, which ends the twice-daily temple sacrifices. This then begins the great tribulation for the Gentiles and Jacob's trouble for the Jewish people.

1 Cor.	1 Corinthians
1 Macc.	1 Maccabees
1 Thess.	1 Thessalonians
1 Tim.	1 Timothy
2 Cor.	2 Corinthians
2 Pet.	2 Peter
2 Thess.	2 Thessalonians
AOD	Abomination of Desolation
Apr.	April
Aug.	August
c.f.	Confer
Dan.	Daniel
Day 1	middle of the seventieth week of Daniel
Day 1,260	end of the seventieth week of Daniel
Dec.	December
Deut.	Deuteronomy
Ex.	Exodus
Ezek.	Ezekiel
ff.	and following
Fri.	Friday
Heb.	Hebrews
Hos.	Hosea
Isa.	Isaiah

Jul.	July
Jun.	June
Lev.	Leviticus
Matt.	Matthew
Mal.	Malachi
Mon.	Monday
Nov.	November
Oct.	October
Rev.	Revelation
Sat.	Saturday
Sep.	September
Sun.	Sunday
T.	Trumpet
Thur.	Thursday
Tue.	Tuesday
W.	These numbered days count from when the two witnesses arrive on earth until they leave earth.
Wed.	Wednesday
Zech.	Zechariah

Definitions

Light: Unless indicated otherwise, this is a normal 24 hour cycle of day and night. See figures 16 and 26.

Darkness: Unless indicated otherwise, this is 24-hour eschatological darkness. They are during the following: part of Day 1 (Zech. 14:6–7), sixth opened seal (Rev. 6:12), fifth blown trumpet (Rev. 9:2), Day 1,253 – 1,254 (Rev. 14:17–19 with parallel Acts 2:17–21), and fifth poured bowl (Rev. 16:10).

Days of Awe: The ten days start with Rosh Hashanah (first fall feast of the Lord) and ends with Yom Kippur (second fall feast of the Lord) are known as the Days of Awe or the Days of Repentance. The is a yearly Jewish event. It foreshadows the coming of the Messiah where all of Israel repents. These ten days are also called days of repentance.

Eschatology: A branch of theology concerned with future biblical end–time prophecy fulfillment, including for example: Christ's second coming, the millennium, and the new earth.

Septet: A septet is a group of seven similar things. In reference to eschatology: seven opened seals, seven blown trumpets, and seven poured bowls. Unless noted otherwise, references to septet will be in relation to these three sets of septets. There are other eschatological septets, such as the seven lampstands – churches (Rev. 2–3), seven thunders (Rev. 10:3), and seven eschatological days of the Lord.

Notes

Figures are not drawn to exact scale.

Unless otherwise noted, all dates are Hebrew, when the day begins after sunset.

Introduction

WATCHMAN ON THE TOWER

I feel like a proverbial watchman on the tower who is among the first to see what appears coming from a far distance away a sword upon the land of Israel and the world. The coming sword is from the Antichrist with Jacob's trouble and the great tribulation. Ezekiel, the watchman, had the responsibility in Ezekiel 33:6 to blow the trumpet of the coming sword or else the loss of life would be the responsibility of the watchman. In a similar way, I feel led to sound the prophetic trumpet of this theory. If the watchman sighting is true, then other watchmen would later confirm it.

OVERVIEW

Four key concepts of this theory include:

1) The seventieth week of Daniel begins: 13 November 2023, 9 November 2026, or 23 October 2063. These dates are each one Jewish day from sunset to sunset, likely measured from Jerusalem. When the seventieth week of Daniel does begin with Daniel 9:27, it means the pretribulation rapture view is no longer viable. At that moment, all should prepare in earnest to live through the fourth and fifth opened seals of tribulation.

2) Specific dates are provided when to hide in your chamber to mitigate the persecution of a *little while* from Isaiah 26:20 fury. *Little while* duration can be determined with Revelation 6:11, John 16:16–18, John 14:19, 16:16, and other Scriptures as 40–46 days. Since this author's previous book determined the duration of the sixth and seventh opened seals and the elect rapture on Tishri 1 or Tishri 2 from *Beyond Prewrath End-Time Prophecy*, it is now possible to determine exact dates when to hide. This fury within the great tribulation will end with an earthquake and 24-hour darkness (Matt. 24:29 and Rev. 6:12).

3) Many teachers and pastors exacerbate not being able to mitigate the persecution in the opened seals. Chapter 12 refutes this.

4) The two witnesses will likely arrive on a Passover five days before Day 1.

An unexpected consequence of examining the fall feasts of the Lord was finding the ten Days of Awe appears to occur concurrently when the sixth and seventh trumpets are blown. This leads to literally assigning specific dates to some Scripture, such as:

   1) *Day 1,251* – Feast of Trumpets where Jesus is seated on a cloud in Revelation 14:14.

   2) *Day 1,253* – The Jews are spiritually saved in Acts 2:17–21 with therefore parallel in Revelation 14:17.

   3) *Day 1,254* – The day of the Lord labeled as the Jehoshaphat battle (Rev. 9:13–19; 14:18–19; Joel 3:2).

   4) *Day 1,260* – Yom Kippur where Israel is raptured in Revelation 11:19.

   For God is not a God of confusion but of peace. As in all the churches of the saints. (1 Cor. 14:33)

FIGURE 1: BEYOND PREWRATH OVERVIEW TIMELINE

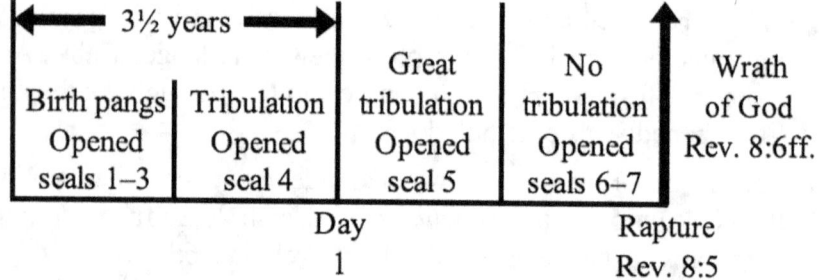

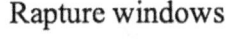

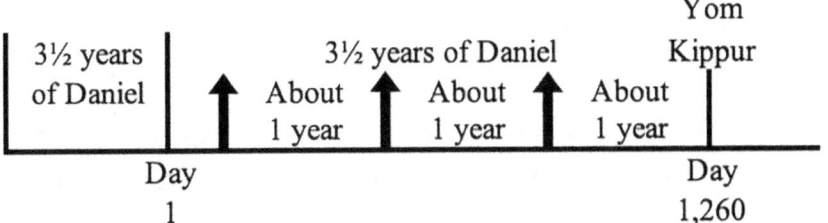

BEYOND PREWRATH PREMILLENNIAL VIEW

The Feast of Trumpets is representative of the eschatological rapture for the elect. This position was put forward in my earlier book *Beyond Prewrath End–Time Prophecy*. Beyond Prewrath was coined since the rapture of the elect is so close to the Prewrath position. An overview of the Beyond Prewrath rapture position follows.

Jesus prophesied in Luke 17:24, "For as the lightning flashes and lights up the sky from one side to the other, so will the Son of Man be in his day." Lightning flashes are proposed as being the method of how the elect will be forcibly taken to meet Jesus in the sky. These lightning flashes were similarly described a few centuries earlier when Elijah was raptured in 2 Kings 2:11, "And as they still went on and talked, behold, chariots of fire and horses of fire separated the two of them. And Elijah went up by a whirlwind into heaven." Chariots and horses of fire is a synonym for lightning. In Revelation 8:5 there are lightning flashes, ". . . there were peals of thunder, rumblings, flashes of lightning, and an earthquake." This same theophany without the earthquake is found in Revelation 4:5. Verses 10–11 indicate the lightning flashes are emanating from the Lord who is seated on the throne.

This same Revelation 8:5 theophany can only be found in Revelation 11:19 and 16:18. These two scriptures were proposed to represent a rapture event for Israel, and the sheep and goats, respectively. Having three rapture events may seem unusual, as it was to me initially, though this is the interpretation which Scripture is pointing us to. The Revelation 11:19 rapture is at end of the seventieth week of Daniel, representative of the current posttribulation view.

We know the separation of the righteous with His rapture (day of Christ) and the wrath of God (day of the Lord) against the wicked are to occur on the same day as with Noah and Lot, so one would expect these two eschatological events described close to each other in Scripture. Revelation 8:5 was previously supported as the rapture of the elect. We see this associated wrath prophesized by Jesus in Luke 17:29 as ". . . fire and sulfur . . ." with it fulfilled in Revelation 8:7 ". . . hail and fire mixed with blood. . . ." These two verses (v. 5 and v. 7) being only two verses apart is representative of a same day type of event.

Revelation 7:9–16 multitude rejoicing in heaven is considered a consequence of the Revelation 8:5 rapture with its earthly theophany. Consider Revelation 7 is not marked as either the sixth or seventh seals. This becomes a non-chronological interpretation of Revelation. We know the entire Bible is not chronological, so this should not be a complete surprise.

These previous paragraphs point to the beyond prewrath view as the following chronological events: Revelation 6 (seals 1 to 6), Revelation 8:1–5 (seal 7 with its earthly rapture of lightning in v. 5 to meet Jesus in the sky), Revelation 7:9–17 (multitude in heaven rejoicing), and then the Lot type of wrath of God in Revelation 8:7. Jesus prophesized this wrath of God by fire in Luke 17:29.

The following are a few of the other new eschatological understandings put forth in the first book *Beyond Prewrath End–Time Prophecy*:

1) The duration of the sixth opened seal was proposed as 27 to 32 days.
2) The duration of the seventh opened seal was proposed. The rapture occurring on either the seventh or eighth day.
3) No tribulation during the sixth or seventh opened seals.
4) 2 Thessalonians 2:1–3 day of the Lord is chronologically applicable to the middle of the seventieth week of Daniel, called Day 1, and not the later same day rapture for the elect.

FALLING AWAY

Clarification is provided to *Beyond Prewrath End–Time Prophecy* on falling away from the faith. 2 Thessalonians 2:1–4 has the falling away to occur before the day of the Lord. This day of the Lord was supported as Day 1. Therefore, this falling away appears to occur before Day 1 by taking the mark of the beast in order to buy and sell. This would fall within the fourth opened seal of tribulation since it ends immediately before Day 1. They are not committed to hades unless they also worship the beast and his image, as the third angel world-wide megaphone warning in Revelation 14:9–11 likely on Day 1.

If you are skeptical of this understanding, then consider that even eleven of the apostles fell away from Jesus on that Passover. They, of course, later recovered their faith and most died as martyrs. The twelfth apostle Judas killed himself.

> Then Jesus said to them, "You will all *fall away* because of me this night. For it is written, 'I will strike the shepherd, and the sheep of the flock will be scattered.' (Matt. 26:31, emphasis added)

THE TRIBULATION VS. SEVENTIETH WEEK OF DANIEL

Many premillennial scholars call the entire seventieth week of Daniel *The Tribulation*. This author disagrees. The tribulation occurs in the fourth opened seal (Matt. 24:9–14 and Rev. 6:7–8) and the great tribulation in the fifth opened seal (Matt. 24:15–26 and Rev. 6:9–11). The tribulation ends with the sixth opened seal in Matthew 24:29 and its parallel in Revelation 6:12.

No matter whether the tribulation ends for one day or significantly longer within the seventieth week of Daniel, the entire seventieth week cannot be called *The Tribulation*. To try to say it is a time of calamity is to introduce a different Scripture meaning.

> Then they will deliver you up to *tribulation* and put you to death, and you will be hated by all nations for my name's sake. (Matt. 24:9, emphasis added)

> For then there will be *great tribulation*, such as has not been from the beginning of the world until now, no, and never will be. (Matt. 24:21, emphasis added)

> *Immediately after the tribulation* of those days the sun will be darkened, and the moon will not give its light, and the stars will fall from heaven, and the powers of the heavens will be shaken. (Matt. 24:29, emphasis added)

FIFTH OPENED SEAL WITH GREAT TRIBULATION START ON DAY 1

The following provides support of the fifth open seal occurring on Day 1. This understanding will later be built on in chapter 7 to support the woman Israel being pursued by the dragon Satan starting on Day 1 in Revelation 12:13–16.

Daniel 9:27 has the abomination occurring in the middle of the seventieth week of Daniel defined as Day 1. This is the same eschatological abomination described in Matthew 24:15. The chronological parallel of Revelation 6:9–11 for the fifth opened seal can be found in Matthew 24:15–26.

The previous four opened seals in Revelation 6:1–8 describe the same parallel events in Matthew 24:4–14, which adds support for this understanding. Chapter 6 of *Beyond Prewrath End–Time Prophecy* goes deeper in supporting this chronology.

Therefore, the fifth opened seal begins on Day 1.

> And he shall make a strong covenant with many for one week, and for *half of the week* he shall put an end to sacrifice and offering. And on the wing of *abominations shall come one who makes desolate*, until the decreed end is poured out on the desolator. (Dan. 9:27, emphasis added)

> So, when you see the *abomination of desolation* spoken of by the prophet Daniel, standing in the holy place (let the reader understand). (Matt. 24:15, emphasis added)

> When he *opened the fifth seal*, I saw under the altar the souls of those who had been slain for the word of God and for the witness they had borne. (Rev. 6:9, emphasis added)

Chapter 1

Feasts of the Lord and Fulfilled Prophecies

SPRING FEASTS

In the Hebrew calendar, there are four spring feasts of the Lord: (1) Passover, (2) Unleavened bread, (3) First Fruits, and (4) Feast of Weeks. Leviticus 23:4 requires these as "the appointed feasts of the Lord, the holy convocations, which you shall proclaim at the time appointed for them." Jesus prophetically fulfilled all of these feasts with the below associated meanings on the exact day and in sequence.

The first spring feast is Passover on Nisan 14 in March or April. Jesus participated with the apostles at the Passover evening meal and then the next day at the ninth hour (3 p.m.) he died on the cross (Mark 15:34–37). Since a Jewish day begins shortly after sunset and ends about 24-hours later, therefore both events were on the Passover. Passover is one of the three major holy convocations in Judaism when they would make a pilgrimage to the temple in Jerusalem.[1] Two other Jewish pilgrimages are Feast of Weeks and Tabernacles, also known as Tents or Booths.[2]

The second spring feast is Unleavened Bread on Nisan 15–21 (Ex. 12:14–20). This feast is representative that Jesus's body would not decay in the grave.[3]

The third spring feast is First Fruits on Nisan 16. Since Jesus was the first resurrected from the grave, He is the first fruits.[4]

The fourth spring feast of the Lord is the Feast of Weeks on Sivan 6 in Leviticus 23:15–16. On this day is also the Christian observance of Pentecost when the Holy Spirit came down in Acts 2:1–4.

---

1 Randal Price, *Rose Book of Bible Charts, Maps & Time Lines*, Rose Publishing, © 2005, 58.
2 Ibid., 58, 60.
3 Kevin Howard and Marvin Rosenthal, *The Feasts of the Lord – God's Prophetic Calendar from Calvary to the Kingdom*, Published in Nashville, Tennessee, by Thomas Nelson, Inc., © 1997, 44.
4 Ibid.

When the day of Pentecost arrived, they were all together in one place. And suddenly there came from heaven a sound like a mighty rushing wind, and it filled the entire house where they were sitting. And divided tongues as of fire appeared to them and rested on each one of them. And they were all filled with the Holy Spirit and began to speak in other tongues as the Spirit gave them utterance. (Acts 2:1–4)

FALL FEASTS

There are three fall feasts of the Lord: (1) Rosh Hashanah/Feast of Trumpets, (2) Yom Kippur/Day of Atonement, and (3) Booths/Tabernacles.

The first fall feast is Rosh Hashanah/Feast of Trumpets is the seventh month of their year. This is celebrated in September or October on Tishri 1. This annual Jewish New Year festival is celebrated by the blowing of the smaller shofar (ram's horn) for a hundred different trumpet blasts during the synagogue services.[5] This is the beginning of the Jewish calendar year. The Lord commanded the Jews to observe this in Leviticus 23:23–25 and Numbers 29:1–6.

The second fall feast is Yom Kippur, also called Day of Atonement on Tishri 10. Day of Atonement is the most solemn holy day of the year in Judaism.[6] It is a time of prayer and fasting on the last day before God's judgment.[7]

The ten days between these first two fall feasts of the Lord are observances called the Days of Awe or Days of Repentance.[8] During these High Holy days, the High Priest would sacrifice an animal for everyone's sins. Since the temple was destroyed in 70 AD, Jewish people substitute good works, charitable gifts, and prayers to atone for their sins.[9] Jews were commanded by the Lord to observe this in Leviticus 16, 23:26–32, and Numbers 29:7–11.

Tabernacles is the third fall feast. It is a seven–day holiday starting on Tishri 15. The Lord commanded the Jews to observe this in Leviticus 23:33–43 and Numbers 29:12–38.

---

5 Randal Price, *Rose Book of Bible Charts, Maps & Time Lines*, Rose Publishing, © 2005, 58.
6 Ibid., 60.
7 Ibid.
8 Ibid., 61.
9 Ibid.

Hanukkah, also called Feast of Dedication, is on Kislev 25. It is not a biblical feast, though we see its importance since Jesus went to the temple in John 10:22–23. Hanukkah is an annual Jewish festival commemorating the rededication of the second temple in Jerusalem during the Maccabean revolt against the Seleucid Greek Empire just over 2,100 years ago.[10] In order to fulfill the prophecy of the temple abomination in Daniel 9:27, a third temple must be built prior to the middle of the seventieth week.

EDGAR C. WHISENANT – RETURN OF CHRIST IN 1988

Those of us who are old enough recognize Edgar C. Whisenant books *88 Reasons Why the Rapture Could be in 1988* and *On Borrowed Time*. He had a pretribulation rapture view which used the fall feasts of the Lord date setting to come up with his second coming of the Lord. The following discusses the main themes of his theory.[11]

He equated the three fall feasts of the Lord with the following eschatological events:

1) First fall feast – Feast of Trumpets as the rapture,

2) Second fall feast – Yom Kippur as both the signing of the Peace Pact by Antichrist at the start of the seventieth week of Daniel and Day 1,260, and

3) Third fall feast – Tabernacles as the arrival of the two witnesses.

Several other scholars[12] equate the three fall feasts to: (1) the rapture of the elect, (2) Day 1,260 (Tishri 10), and (3) Day 1,265 (Tishri 15), respectively. So, there is agreement with the first feast of the Lord associated with a rapture event. His second fall feast interpretation is correct for Day 1,260,

---

10 Ibid., 60.
11 Edgar C. Whisenant, *On Borrowed Time*, World Bible Society, New Expanded Edition, © 1988, 5.
12 A few scholars have already breached this subject of assigning eschatological meaning to the fall feasts of the Lord with the same interpretation. Some of these scholars include Marvin Rosenthal, *The Feasts of the Lord*; Sam Nadler, *Messiah in the Feasts of Israel*; Michael Norten, *Unlocking the Secrets of the Feasts*; Bruce Booker, *The Feasts of the Lord*; and Robert van Kampen, *The Sign of Christ's Coming and the End of the Age*.

though it will be shown incorrect as the start of the seventieth week.[13] His third fall feast interpretation is incorrect.

He also correctly equated Jerusalem 70 AD destruction by the Romans as part of the Matthew 24:1–3 prophecy fulfillment of the first generation.

> Jesus left the temple and was going away, when his disciples came to point out to him the buildings of the temple. But he answered them, "You see all these, do you not? Truly, I say to you, there will not be left here one stone upon another that will not be thrown down." (Matt. 24:1–2)

EDGAR C. WHISENANT – THEORY FLAWS

One of his main flaws was assuming the Jewish lifespan of about forty years in 70 AD is the same as it will be with Jesus second coming.[14] This author does agree that using 14 May 1948 as the chronological start date of the second generation has the best merit. Chapter 9 discusses that in 70 AD, the Jewish lifespan in Israel would be raised significantly when compared to other countries of that era as a consequence of the apostles healing a massive number of mostly Jews (Matt. 10:1–8; 19:13; Acts 5:12–16). The age determination method of the first–generation then helps to define what the second–generation age should be. This second–generation age will be shown in chapter 9 to be about twice as long.

> Truly, I say to you, this *generation* will not pass away until all these things take place. (Matt. 24:34, emphasis added)

A second flaw is that he equated Yom Kippur with the start of the seventieth week of Daniel.[15] Since the Jewish calendar is both solar and lunar, this rarely if ever occurs. Yom Kippur in 1988 was 20 September and in 1995 on 4 October. To confirm whether this is possible as the start and end of the seventieth week of Daniel they must be separated by exactly seven of Daniel years minus one for counting, or 2,519 days. That is, seven times 360 then minus one. Yom Kippur 1988 to Yom Kippur 1995 is a difference

---

13 Edgar C. Whisenant, *88 Reasons Why the Rapture Could be in 1988*, New Expanded Edition, © 1988, 19.
14 Ibid., 9–10.
15 Ibid., 19.

of 2,570 days and not the required 2,519 days. This demonstrates his logic was incorrect that the start of the seventieth week started on a Yom Kippur.

Another flaw is that he has a pretribulation rapture position where the rapture occurs at the start of the seventieth week of Daniel. This author has a Beyond Prewrath premillennial position with the rapture of the elect occurring in second half of Daniel's seventieth week at the end of the seventh opened seal with Revelation 8:5.

Chapter 2

Future Fall Feast Prophecies

FALL FEASTS FULFILLED IN SEQUENCE

Since the associated events of the spring feasts of the Lord were prophetically fulfilled on the same day and in sequence, the fall feasts of the Lord could also have similar prophetic meaning. We know our God is not a God of confusion but of peace, so this warrants further investigation.

So, what are the future prophetic events associated with these fall feasts of the Lord? A few scholars have already almost universally agreed to what they are as described below.[1]

FIRST FALL FEAST – ROSH HASHANAH/FEAST OF TRUMPETS

Points to the future day when the Messiah returns to rescue the righteous with the rapture and judge the wicked.[2] This future day for the righteous in Titus 2:13 is called the "Blessed Hope," since believers will have a physical rapture and others a resurrection from the grave. Also, consider Michael Norten's book *Unlocking the Secrets of the Feasts* in which he describes many of his discussions with Messianic Jews who said: "Of course the rapture will happen at Rosh Hashanah!"[3] The Bible verses below point to the trumpet being blown during the rapture.

> [He] will send out his angels with a loud *trumpet* call, and they will gather his elect from the four winds, from one end of heaven to the other. (Matt. 24:31, emphasis added)

---

1 See chapter 1, footnote 12.
2 Kevin Howard and Marvin Rosenthal, *The Feasts of the Lord – God's Prophetic Calendar from Calvary to the Kingdom,* Published in Nashville, Tennessee, by Thomas Nelson, Inc., 1997, 44.
3 Michael Norten, *Unlocking the Secrets of the Feasts – The Prophecies in the Feasts of Leviticus*, West Bow Press, 2012, 54.

[The] Lord himself will descend from heaven with a cry of command, with the voice of an archangel, and with the sound of the *trumpet* of God. And the dead in Christ will rise first. Then we who are alive, who are left, will be caught up together with them in the clouds to meet the Lord in the air, and so we will always be with the Lord. Therefore encourage one another with these words. (1 Thess. 4:16–18, emphasis added)

Behold! I tell you a mystery. We shall not all sleep, but we shall all be changed, in a moment, in the twinkling of an eye, at the *last trumpet*. For the *trumpet* will sound, and the dead will be raised imperishable, and we shall be changed. (1 Cor. 15:51–52, emphasis added)

SECOND FALL FEAST – YOM KIPPUR/DAY OF ATONEMENT

Yom Kippur was the only day of the year when the high priest would enter the Holy of Holies in the innermost chamber of the temple or tabernacle to make atonement for the sins of all Israel (Lev. 16:34). Today, the ten days from Rosh Hashanah to Yom Kippur are days of repentance, also called Days of Awe, when Jews express remorse for their sins through prayer and fasting.[4]

Zechariah 12:8–10 shows the future prophecy of their mourning, repentance, and the day of the Lord's salvation. This points to the future day when Israel repents of her sins and turns to the Messiah for salvation.[5] Daniel 9:24 points to this future day of Israel's atonement. Israel's spiritual salvation appears to occur in Acts 2:17–21 during these ten days of Awe. In Revelation 12:6 and 13–14, Israel flees on Day 1 with the interpreted same day AOD in Daniel 9:27, and is protected for 1,260 days. Israel being raptured in Revelation 11:19 on that last day is reflective of when it ends.

---

4 Randal Price, *Rose Book of Bible Charts, Maps & Time Lines*, Rose Publishing, © 2005, 60–61.

5 Kevin Howard and Marvin Rosenthal, *The Feasts of the Lord – God's Prophetic Calendar from Calvary to the Kingdom*, Published in Nashville, Tennessee, by Thomas Nelson, Inc., 1997, 44.

On that day the LORD will protect the inhabitants of Jerusalem, so that the feeblest among them on that day shall be like David, and the house of David shall be like God, like the angel of the LORD, going before them. And on that day I will seek to destroy all the nations that come against Jerusalem. "And I will pour out on the house of David and the inhabitants of Jerusalem a spirit of grace and pleas for mercy, so that, when they look on me, on him whom they have pierced, they shall mourn for him, as one mourns for an only child, and weep bitterly over him, as one weeps over a firstborn. (Zech. 12:8–10)

Seventy weeks are decreed about your people and your holy city, to finish the transgression, to put an end to sin, and to *atone* for iniquity, to bring in everlasting righteousness, to seal both vision and prophet, and to anoint a most holy place. (Dan. 9:24, emphasis added)

[T]he *woman* (Israel) fled into the wilderness, where she has a place prepared by God, in which she is to be nourished for *1,260 days*. (Rev. 12:6, emphasis added)

[W]hen the *dragon* (Satan) saw that he had been thrown down to the earth, he pursued the *woman* (Israel) who had given birth to the male child. But the woman was given the two wings of the great eagle so that she might fly from the serpent into the wilderness, to the place where she is to be nourished for *a time (one year), and times (two years), and half a time (half a year)* (total of 1,260 days). (Rev. 12:13–14, emphasis added)

THIRD FALL FEAST – FEAST OF TABERNACLES/BOOTHS/SUKKOT

Feast of Tabernacles is the third fall feast from Tishri 15 to 21. This is the future day when our Messiah sets up the messianic Kingdom and tabernacles among men.[6] During the millennium this will be celebrated yearly in Jerusalem.

---

6 Ibid.

HANUKKAH – FEAST OF DEDICATION

Hanukkah is a rededication celebration of the second temple to the Lord, which has been celebrated for over 2,100 years since it was desecrated by the Gentiles (Dan. 8:9–14; Ezra 6:16). The cleansing and dedication of the temple is described in 1 Maccabees 4:36–61.[7] In a similar way the next (third) temple will be desecrated as described in Daniel 9:27 and Matthew 24:15. Then later in the millennium a fourth temple rededication would occur as with previous Hanukkahs (Rev. 21).

---

7 The Apocrypha of the Old Testament, 1611 King James Version, American Bible Society, New York.

Chapter 3

History of the Feasts of the Lord Theory

The following shows the history from the Prewrath position to the Beyond Prewrath position. We will start off with the basic Prewrath position in the third row of figure 3. This figure shows one upward arrow representing a rapture date in the second half of the seventieth week of Daniel. Both the Prewrath and Beyond Prewrath positions are chronologically so close that only one upward arrow is shown.

Prewrath has their rapture in Revelation 7:9–17 (if not just before) with the rejoicing in heaven. Beyond prewrath has the elect rapture in Revelation 8:5 with a great eschatological theophany of "Peals of thunder, rumblings, flashes of lightning, and an earthquake." Then the consequence of the earthly rapture is Revelation 7:9–17 rejoicing in heaven. Therefore, the book of Revelation is proposed as not being chronological.

FIGURE 3: FIVE RAPTURE POSITIONS

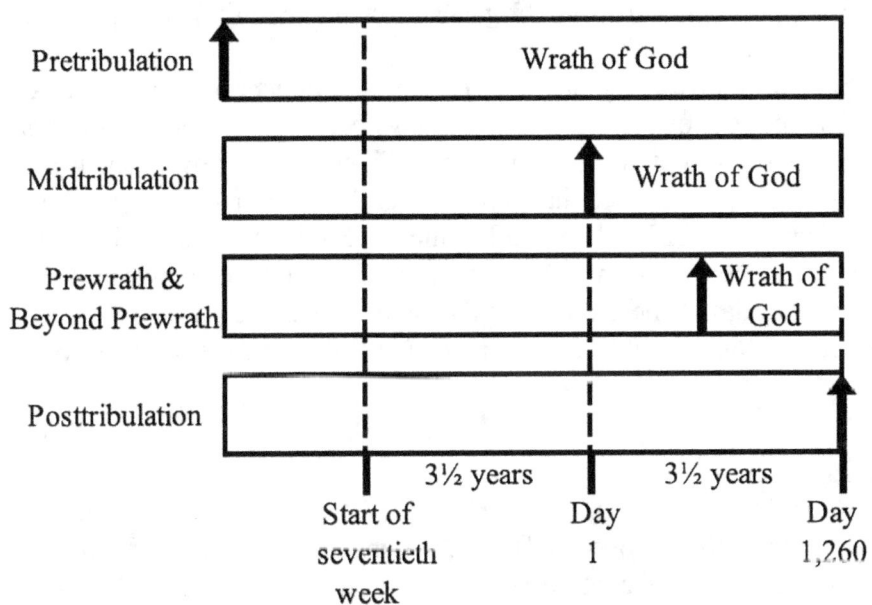

EARLY PREWRATH WITH FALL FEASTS

The Sign of Christ's Coming and the End of the Age published in 1992 by Robert Van Kampen conceptually presented the prewrath position with the feasts of the Lord.[1] He has the covenant of Daniel 9:27 being signed 2,519 days prior to the eschatological Yom Kippur at the end of the seventieth week, which uses a Daniel year as 360 days.[2] He included the second and third fall feasts of the Lord in the timeline and he also included Hanukkah as 75 days after Day 1,260. Though he did not include the first fall feast, which the Beyond Prewrath theory represents as the rapture of the elect.

THE LAST SHOFAR!

The authors Joseph Lenard & Donald Zoller book *The Last Shofar! What the Fall Feasts of the Lord are Telling the Church* was published 2014 using the feasts of the Lord to understanding the seventieth week of Daniel.[3] Two things are incorrect with this theory.[4]

First, it is not possible to have Yom Kippur as the start and end of the seventieth week of Daniel since a prophetic year of Daniel is 360 days versus our 365 or 366 days in a year. Edgar Whisenant had this same theory, which was disproved in chapter 1.

Second, their theory has the Feast of Trumpets on Tishri 1 as exactly one Daniel year of 360 days and ten days earlier from the Yom Kippur at the end of the seventieth week of Daniel. Since the Hebrew calendar is lunar and solar based this rarely happens, if ever. For example, consider the Feast of Trumpets for Tishri 1 in 2022, which is 5 October. Yom Kippur would occur in the next year on 16 September 2023. Difference between these two dates is 346 days. Therefore, their theory of 360 and ten days does not equal the actual 346 days. This is a second example that this theory does not work.

---

1   Robert Van Kampen, *The Sign of Christ's Coming and the End of the Age*, Published by Crossway Books, a publishing ministry of Good News Publishers, 1300 Crescent Street, Wheaton, Illinois 60187, 1992, 474.
2   Ibid., 476.
3   Joseph Lenard & Donald Zoller, *The Last Shofar! What the Feasts of the Lord are Telling the Church*, Xulon Press, 2014, xix.
4   Ibid., 118, 129, 145, and 210.

NUMBER OF POSSIBLE RAPTURE WINDOWS IN SECOND HALF OF DANIEL

How many annual Feast of Trumpets (Tishri 1 in September or October) are celebrated between the middle and end of the seventieth week of Daniel? Since Day 1,260 (Yom Kippur) is always in September or October that points to Day 1 as April or early May.

There are three annual two–day rapture window dates in which the rapture of the Church could be prophetically fulfilled. A fourth upward pointing arrow just prior to the end of the seventieth week of Daniel is not possible considering the later fifth blown trumpet is 150 days long in Revelation 9:5 and must occur before Day 1,260, though after the rapture of the elect. Therefore, a fourth upward arrow representing a possible rapture event will not be shown.

CONCLUSION

Compiling this information, leads to a new theory in figure 4 as to when the rapture of the elect could occur. Each upward arrow represents an annual window, where any of these could fulfill prophecy for the rapture. According to Jewish tradition the Feast of Trumpets lasts for two days. So, the Jewish New Year's feast would last for two consecutive days.[5] These two successive days fit well with *Beyond Prewrath End–Time Prophecy* chapter 3 of the opened seventh seal rapture on either the seventh or eighth day. That is, when we leave the daily 24–hour darkness of the opened sixth seal and enter into the "light" (normal day and night) of the opened seventh seal, then the rapture occurs on either the seventh or eighth day.

---

5 Alfred Edersheim, *The Temple – Its Ministry and Services As They Were at the Time of Jesus Christ*, Kregel Publications, Grand Rapids, MI 49501, © 1997, 138–139.

FIGURE 4: RAPTURE WINDOWS OF THE ELECT

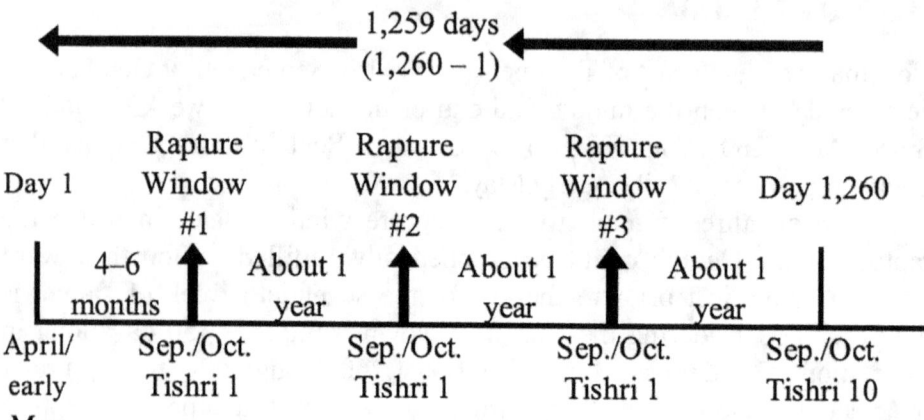

Chapter 4

Identify the Start of the Seventieth Week of Daniel

If this theory is correct, then we can determine various dates when the beginning of the seventieth prophetic week may happen. When it does happen, we will be alert for coming false prophets and prepare ourselves for what will happen over the next several years. In order to fulfill the start of Daniel 9:27 last prophetic week, a Daniel seven–year agreement with many countries, must be signed on the expected day. Since many countries sign the covenant, then when does it become binding? Perhaps once Israel signs it and at least one other country. Caution is advised that the actual date may be misrepresented as before or after. Berean wisdom may be needed.

This day is 2,519 days before the end of the expected seventieth week of Daniel. 2,519 days is derived by multiplying seven of Daniel years by 360 days per year then subtracting one–day when counting chronologically backward from Yom Kippur on Day 1,260. This end of Daniel's seventieth week in chapter 2 equated to a Yom Kippur date. Isaiah 28:15 describes this agreement as a covenant with death.

Some may use Matthew 24:36–39 to say no one can know this date, though this Scripture is applicable only to the rapture of the elect.

> But concerning that day and hour no one knows, not even the angels of heaven, nor the Son, but the Father only . . . so will be the coming of the Son of Man. (Matt. 24:36–39)

Figure 5 forms the basis of this theory. The abomination of desolation (AOD), occurs on Day 1 with Daniel 9:27. Figure 6 provides a few of these annual years. Filters are provided in later chapters which narrow down this list of annual possible dates.

> And he shall make a strong covenant with many for one week, and for half of the week he shall put an end to sacrifice and offering. And on the wing of abominations shall come one who makes desolate, until the decreed end is poured out on the desolator. (Dan. 9:27)

FIGURE 5: SEVENTIETH WEEK OF DANIEL

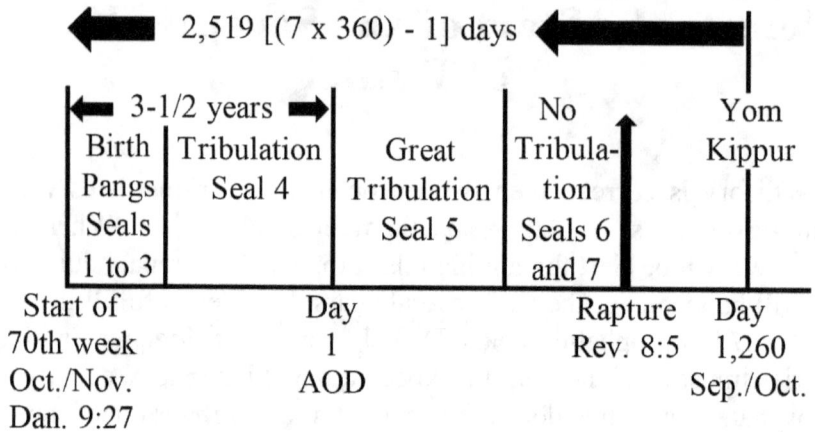

FIGURE 6: SEVENTIETH WEEK OF DANIEL WITH DATES

Yom Kippur (Day 1,260)	Start of 70th week (2,519 Days before Yom Kippur)
9/20/2026	10/28/2019
10/10/2027	11/16/2020
9/29/2028	11/6/2021
9/18/2029	10/26/2022
10/6/2030	11/13/2023
9/26/2031	11/2/2024
9/14/2032	10/22/2025
10/2/2033	11/9/2026
9/22/2034	10/30/2027
9/15/2070	10/23/2063

CONCLUSION

Christians should be observant of a possible seven–year multi–national agreement with Israel occurring during one of these figure 6 yearly dates.

Identify the Start of the Seventieth Week of Daniel 23

Consider, once we hear that this agreement has been signed on one of the specific annual dates, we can then confidently eliminate the earlier pretribulation rapture position as a viable position. This is since Daniel 9:27 says the signed treaty starts the seventieth week of Daniel. Each 24-hour Jewish day begins just after sunset when three stars become visible in the night sky with the geographical focus being Jerusalem. The rest of the world uses midnight as their new day.

Chapter 5

Determine Rapture Window Dates

In order for the Lord to fulfill prophecy for this theory, he must return to meet the elect in the sky, during one of the three annual Feast of Trumpets in figure 8. Is a fourth annual rapture window possible? On the Mount of Olives, Jesus said in Matthew 24:22, "And if those days had not been cut short, no human being would be saved. But for the sake of the elect those days will be cut short." This is a strong statement about cutting short the duration of the great tribulation.

According to this theory, the great tribulation must be shortened from one of these dates to another earlier date. No human surviving would indicate the great tribulation being cut short more than one day of the fourth rapture two-day window date. If it is cut short more than a day, then the next increment it could be cut short would be about a year. Therefore, Matthew 24:22 seems it must be cut short at least one year. The rapture of the elect being shorten by at least one year would indicate a significant amount of time to end the persecution.

The question then becomes, is the persecution being cut short from a fourth annual rapture window or from the third annual rapture window? I have taken the conservative view that it is being cut short from the fourth rapture window date. So, there becomes three separate two-day annual possible rapture window dates.

FIGURE 7: RAPTURE WINDOWS OF THE ELECT

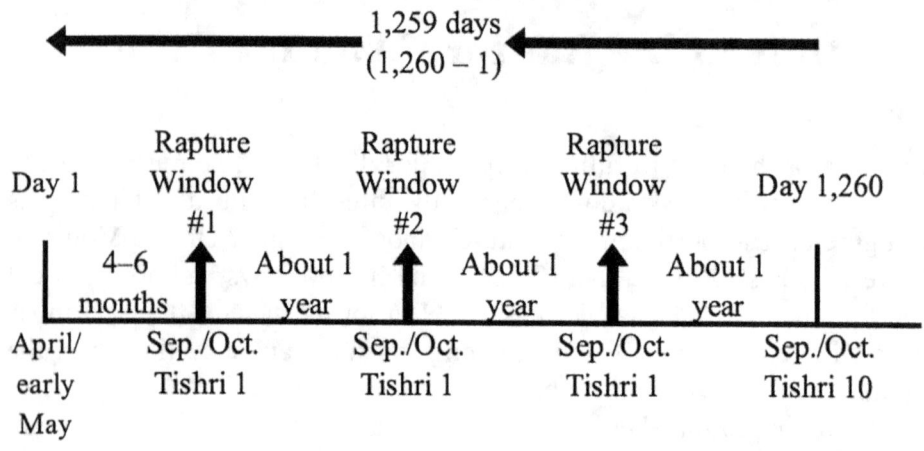

FIGURE 8: RAPTURE WINDOW START DATES FOR TISHRI 1

Day 1	First yearly window	Second yearly window	Third yearly window
10 Apr. 2023	15 Sep. 2023	2 Oct. 2024	22 Sep. 2025
29 Apr. 2024	2 Oct. 2024	22 Sep. 2025	11 Sep. 2026
19 Apr. 2025	22 Sep. 2025	11 Sep. 2026	1 Oct. 2027
8 Apr. 2026	11 Sep. 2026	1 Oct. 2027	20 Sep. 2028
26 Apr. 2027	1 Oct. 2027	20 Sep. 2028	9 Sep. 2029
15 Apr. 2028	20 Sep. 2028	9 Sep. 2029	27 Sep. 2030
4 Apr. 2029	9 Sep. 2029	27 Sep. 2030	17 Sep. 2031
22 Apr. 2030	27 Sep. 2030	17 Sep. 2031	5 Sep. 2032
5 Apr. 2067	9 Sep. 2067	26 Sep. 2068	15 Sep. 2069

NO ONE KNOWS THE DAY

This analysis does not specify a specific day when the rapture of the elect will happen in agreement with what Jesus said in the Olivet Discourse of Matthew 24:36. It does provide three yearly two-day windows when the prophecy may be fulfilled, which is based on the Feasts of the Trumpets having eschatological rapture meaning. In 1 Thessalonians 5:4 we see that for Christians this day will not surprise us.

Once we leave the 24-hour darkness of the sixth open seal (Rev. 6:12; Matt. 24:29), we will enter the seventh open seal. This last opened seal must have a normal night-day, 24-hour cycle. Night is prophesized in Luke 17:34 with two in bed and one taken. Day is prophesized in Luke 17:28 with planting and building, which are normally performed during daylight. The rapture would occur on either the seventh or eighth day after leaving the 24-hour darkness. *Beyond Prewrath End–Time Prophecy* chapter 3 duration of the opened seventh seal of seven or eight days provides a match to each two-day Church rapture window.

Some may discount this theory since the exact moment of when the sliver of moon occurs is now known scientifically. In ancient days it was significantly more difficult to determine this.[1] Consider this sliver of moon, which starts Tishri 1, can be changed since this is the Lord who changed other historical scriptural solar and lunar events.

1) The "LORD, who brought the shadow back ten steps after it had gone down the stairway" (2 Kings 20:1–11; cf. Isa. 38:8). This indicates the rotation of the earth on its axis seems to have been reversed.

2) The sun stood still, and the moon stopped for the Joshua battle in Joshua 10:13. The moon being stopped could affect the earth's shadow on the moon. This could change when a Jewish month begins with its sliver of moon shadow.

3) The Lord created the heavens and all. Nothing is beyond his reach.

NO ONE KNOWS THE HOUR

From *Beyond Prewrath End–Time Prophecy* chapter 3, we saw a great eschatological theophany in Revelation 8:5 occurs with the elect rapture. It is interesting to note that since no one knows the hour of Jesus's return, then the duration of this theophany must also be unknowable. That is once the great eschatological theophany (thunder, lightning flashings, and rumblings) starts, the rapture may not occur within the first hour and may not even

---

1 Kevin Howard and Marvin Rosenthal, *The Feasts of the Lord: God's Prophetic Calendar from Calvary to the Kingdom* (Nashville: Thomas Nelson, 1997), 28.

occur in the first window day of the possible seventh day in the seventh opened seal.

> But concerning that day and hour no one knows, not even the angels of heaven, nor the Son, but the Father only. (Matt. 24:36)

> But you, brethren, are not in darkness, that the day would overtake you like a thief; For you are all children of light, children of the day. We are not of the night or of the darkness. (1 Thess. 5:4–5)

CONCLUSION

Three elect rapture window yearly dates were determined based on the feast of the Lord theory. The third rapture annual window two-day date could be excluded if a less conservative approach is taken. Each yearly window is two days during the second half of the seventieth week of Daniel. These two days range from early September to early October.

Chapter 6

Filter #1, Two Thousand Years Are Two Days

PURPOSE

To examine the 6,000- and 2,000-year methods of determining when Jesus may return.

JEWISH CALENDAR

Most scholars recognize the Jewish calendar is inaccurate. One source has the calendar missing 240 years.[1] From 19 September 2020 to 7 September 2021 the Hebrew year was 5781.[2] Considering 5781 is 219 years from six thousand this would deem the first analysis of missing 240 years as being too high.

Mitchell First *Jewish History in Conflict: A Study of the Major Discrepancy between Rabbinic and Conventional Chronology* documents the following discrepancies,[3] which total 171 to 172 years. All rabbinic chronology is based on the authoritative work of Seder Olam Rabbah. This limited long-range analysis indicates that the return of the Jewish Messiah may be within the next 48 years (219 – 171).

1) <u>155 Years (207 – 52)</u>: In the Persian periods there is a discrepancy of 155 years, where the conventional chronology spans 207 years (539 to 332 BCE) though the Seder Olam Rabbah view only spans 52 years. The 207 years include the following Persian reigns: Cyrus,

---

1   J. R. Church, "The Jewish Calendar's 240 Missing Years" in the magazine *Prophecy in the News*, https://prophecyinthenews.com/ (Oklahoma City, OK: Volume 25, Number 8, August 2005), 4.
2   Hebcal.com, "Jewish Holidays 2020–2021", accessed March 28, 2021, https://www.hebcal.com/holidays/2020 and "Jewish Holidays 2021–2022", https://www.hebcal.com/holidays/2021.
3   Mitchell First, *Jewish History in Conflict: A Study of the Major Discrepancy between Rabbinic and Conventional Chronology*, 1997, xix, 5–6, 161, 164, 171.

nine years; Cambyses, eight years; Darius I, 36 years; Xerxes, 21 years; Artaxerxes I, 41 years; Darius II, 19 years; Artaxerxes II, 46 years; Ochus, 21 years; Arogus, two years; and Darius III, four years. These kings reigned for at least a year, though a few others reigned for less than a year.

2) <u>15 Years</u>: Regarding the Roman, Greek, and Hasmonean period, there is an additional fifteen-year discrepancy.

3) <u>1 or 2 Years</u>: These years are regarding the destruction of the second temple.

JEWISH JUBILEE

The Lord required the jubilee observance every 50 years in Leviticus 25:8–22. Though the Jews have not been scripturally observing any jubilees since at least 70 AD and probably for a few centuries prior to going into Babylonian captivity. Leviticus 25:9 jubilee celebration says, "Then you shall sound the loud trumpet on the tenth day of the seventh month. On the Day of Atonement, you shall sound the trumpet throughout all your land." As we know, the two-thousand-year prophecy would occur on a date, which is divisible by fifty.

TWO THOUSAND YEARS

Another analytical method is to use two thousand years as being two prophetic days, which is representative of Hosea 6:1–2. If so, what would be considered the start date? In the past some used Jesus's birth date. Harold W. Hoehne*w Chronological Aspects of the Life of Christ Jesus* the evidence would lead one to conclude that Christ's birth occurred sometime in late 5 BC or early 4 BC.[4] If this was applied, then two thousand years later would have already occurred on about 1997. So, this prophecy date analysis is not viable.

There are two viable start dates for consideration. One analysis is based on when the temple was destroyed in 70 AD. Two thousand years later would then be the year 2070 for Day 1,260 as discussed in chapter 12. The second analysis is based on when Christ was crucified, as will be discussed next.

---

[4] Harold W. Hoehner, *Chronological Aspects of the Life of Christ*, 1973, 25.

> Come, let us return to the Lord;
>   for he has torn us, that he may heal us;
>   he has struck us down, and he will bind us up.
> After two days he will revive us;
>   on the third day he will raise us up,
>   that we may live before him. (Hos. 6:1–2)

> But do not overlook this one fact, beloved, that with the Lord one day is as a thousand years, and a thousand years as one day. (2 Pet. 3:8)

WHEN WAS JESUS'S CRUCIFIXION?

First consider who crucified Jesus. "So he (Pilate) delivered him (Jesus) over to them to be crucified" (John 19:16). Pontius Pilate served Rome as prefect (governor) of Judea between 26–36 AD for ten years.[5] He presided over the trial of Jesus and delivered Him for execution to satisfy the crowd in Mark 15:15. Harold Hoehner in *Chronological Aspects of the Life of Christ* narrowed down these possible years by using several astronomical studies. These studies indicate as to which years Nisan 14 fell on a Friday when Jesus was crucified.[6] The studies showed the years 27 AD, 30 AD, 33 AD, and 36 AD as probable years of His crucifixion. By using the ministry of Jesus, Hoehner further narrowed this down to either 30 AD or 33 AD.[7] Of these two dates, his most viable date was 33 AD.[8]

Another way to determine when the two thousand years will end is to examine when Jesus was born, then add his 30 years of age, and then add the duration of his ministry (36 months+). *The War on Christmas* by Bodie Hodge has Circa 4 BC as his birth.[9] If we add 33 years, that takes us to his last year on earth as possibly 30 AD. Remember in counting years there is no 0 AD or 0 BC.

---

5 Ibid., 97–98.
6 Ibid., 98–99.
7 Ibid., 99–100.
8 Ibid., 114.
9 Bodie Hodge, "The War on Christmas – Battles in Faith, Tradition and Religious Expression", 2013, 32.

So, we have a double emphasis on 30 AD and 33 AD. These two "yes" responses in figure 9 are emphasized to indicate these double specificity dates.

360 DAYS IN A YEAR FOR A ONE THOUSAND YEARS?

Consider whether each year, within the one thousand years, is measured as 360 days as Daniel's seventy prophetic weeks are. If so, then each year about 5.24 days are lost. Over two thousand years about 10,480 days are lost or about 28.7 years would need accounting for, making the duration about 1971 years (2000 – 28.7). Considering that Pontius Pilate's last year as governor of Judea was 36 AD, adding 1971 years to 36 AD gives an expected Day 1,260 date of 2007 AD. As of August 2022, the Church has not been raptured so the logic of trying to equate 360 days to a year for each one thousand-year increment is not viable.

Hebrew calendar details of the calendar adjustments needed to keep it in alignment with the solar year have been lost.[10] So, for us to try and recreate their historic calendar adequately enough for Bible eschatology use seems impractical. The logical conclusion is to use what our science already considers a year as about 365.24 days.

CONCLUSION

Hosea 6:1–2 has two thousand years representative of two days. If the start date is applicable with Jesus's crucifixion, then we could expect his Day 1,260 return by 2036. That is, two thousand years plus 36 AD. If the start date is applicable with the temple destruction in 70 AD, then his Day 1,260 return may not be until 2070.

The first generation was about 40 years. By about 2030, the second-generation life span age is about twice that. If there is a medical advancement by 2070 it could raise this to 103 years, which opens 2070 as a possibility.

---

10 Kevin Howard and Marvin Rosenthal, "The Feasts of the Lord–God's Prophetic Calendar from Calvary to the Kingdom," Published in Nashville, Tennessee, by Thomas Nelson, Inc., 1997, 41.

FIGURE 9: TWO THOUSAND–YEAR RETURN OF JESUS

Jesus's crucifixion year?	Add 2000 years	Possible year of Day 1,260?
26	2026	No
27	2027	Yes
28	2028	No
29	2029	No
30	2030	*Yes*
31	2031	No
32	2032	No
33	2033	*Yes*
34	2034	No
35	2035	No
36	2036	Yes

Chapter 7

Filter #2, Two Witnesses Arrive on a Passover

PURPOSE

To examine whether the arrive of the two witnesses could occur on a Jewish Passover per the Jewish tradition of leaving an empty place setting for Elijah. To determine the chronological relationship to Day 1.

WHAT ARE THEIR NAMES?

We know one of the two witnesses as the prophet Elijah in Malachi 4:5. Many scholars think the second witness is Moses who represents the law. He was present during the transfiguration with Jesus and Elijah in Matthew 17:1–3. The day of the Lord in Malachi 4:5 is considered the same eschatological day of the Lord as in 2 Thessalonians 2:1–2.

> Behold, I will send you Elijah the prophet before the great and awesome day of the LORD comes. (Mal. 4:5)

> Now concerning the coming of our Lord Jesus Christ and our being gathered together to him, we ask you, brothers, not to be quickly shaken in mind or alarmed, either by a spirit or a spoken word, or a letter seeming to be from us, to the effect that the day of the Lord has come. (2 Thess. 2:1–2)

WITNESSES ARRIVE BEFORE THE DAY OF THE LORD

Many scholars say this day of the Lord referenced in 2 Thessalonians 2:1–4 is the same day the rapture occurs. This author disagrees. By equating these two events on the same day, they are saying the apostle Paul may enter this eschatological day of the Lord and miss the earlier rapture. The thought of Paul entering this day of Lord and missing the same day rapture should be completely baseless. So, how can Paul possibly enter this 2 Thessalonians 2:1–4 day of the Lord and not miss the rapture? The only reasonable solution is that this is a reference to an earlier and separate eschatological day of the

Lord. In fact, there appears to be seven eschatological days of the Lord as supported in *Beyond Prewrath End–Time Prophecy* chapter 8 with overview in figure 28.

Apostle Paul was located in Corinth about eight hundred miles from Jerusalem during his second missionary journey. There was tribulation of believers occurring (2 Cor. 11:24–18; Acts 13:48–52; 14:5–6). It seems possible they were asking the question whether their tribulation had become the eschatological great tribulation. If they were in Jerusalem, they would be able to confirm themselves whether the temple abomination had occurred, therefore starting the great tribulation (Dan. 9:27; Matt. 24:15–16).

This day of the Lord in 2 Thessalonians 2:1–4 is proposed as the Jerusalem battle on Day 1 (Zech. 14:1–12) when Gog attacks in Ezekiel 38. This same Day 1 is when Jesus counter attacks in Zechariah 14:12, which is expected to slow down the great tribulation, though it will not stop it. Another reason it would be slowed down is the same day three angel worldwide warning of Revelation 14:6–11. Jesus will cut it short in Matthew 24:22 as confirmed by the 24-hour darkness and great earthquake of Matthew 24:29 and Revelation 6:12.

PASSOVER ARRIVAL DATE

My first thought in considering whether the witnesses could arrive during a Jewish Passover was the recognition that the Passover was in the early spring and Yom Kippur was in the early fall, which would be a separation of about six months. If we then added three more Daniel years, we are conceivably very close to the 1,260 days the witnesses prophesied, plus a few other days as described in Revelation 11:7–13. So, the rough math indicated it was worth further investigation.

The Jewish tradition of leaving an empty Seder place setting for Elijah or the guest of honor also provided a logical fit. So, a spreadsheet with three columns of data was created with figure 10 for: (1) the annual Passovers, (2) the annual Yom Kippur three calendar years later, and (3) then counting chronologically backward 1,259 days from each respective annual Yom Kippur on Day 1,260 date to equate to the earlier Day 1.

Adding a fourth column, the difference was taken between each yearly Passover (first column) and Day 1 (third column) to determine which event occurred first for each year and the difference in days. To my surprise, figure 10 showed that all the yearly Passovers were before each associated Day 1, since the difference (B − A) was always positive. The only differences

Filter #2, Two Witnesses Arrive on a Passover 37

in the years from 2023 to 2050 were five, six, seven, 35 or 36 days, with the majority of years having five- and seven-day differences. If the two witnesses do arrive on one of the yearly Passovers, this analysis will show those years with a five-day difference is more likely. All rows in figure 10 were selected to support the second Israel generation from 14 May 1948, except the last row which supports 7 June 1967 when Israel took ownership of the temple mount.

FIGURE 10: TWO WITNESSES – CHECKING ASSUMPTION

Passover (A)	Yom Kippur (Day 1,260)	Day 1 (B)	Difference in days (B – A)
4/5/23	9/20/26	4/10/23	5
4/22/24	10/10/27	4/29/24	7
4/12/25	9/29/28	4/19/25	7
4/1/26	9/18/29	4/8/26	7
4/21/27	10/6/30	4/26/27	5
4/10/28	9/26/31	4/15/28	5
3/30/29	9/14/32	4/4/29	5
4/17/30	10/2/33	4/22/30	5
4/7/31	9/22/34	4/12/31	5
3/26/32	10/12/35	5/1/32	36
4/13/33	9/30/36	4/20/33	7
4/3/34	9/18/37	4/8/34	5
4/23/35	10/8/38	4/28/35	5
4/11/36	9/27/39	4/16/36	5
3/30/37	9/16/40	4/6/37	7
4/19/38	10/4/41	4/24/38	5
4/8/39	9/23/42	4/13/39	5
3/28/40	10/13/43	5/2/40	35
3/31/67	9/15/70	4/5/67	5

The following discusses supporting reasons for the two witnesses arriving on a Passover and leaving on Day 1,259. They appear to arrive five days before Day 1 based on a five-day (W1 to W6) timeline as shown in figure 11.

FIRST – PROTECTION FOR 1,260 DAYS

In Revelation 12:6 we see the woman Israel flees the dragon Satan into the wilderness. There in the desert she will be protected and provided for 1,260 days (Rev. 12:13–14). These 1,260 days is placed in the second half of Daniel's seventieth week. The abomination of destruction and great tribulation begins on Day 1 in Daniel 9:27 and Matthew 24:15–21. Many Jews starting on Day 1 will go into exile (Zech. 14:2). For the remnant who are protected for 1,260 days, we can then expect something will happen to occur before their protection ends and possible harm occurs. This something is their physical rapture in Revelation 11:19 with the second great eschatological theophany with its lightning flashes.

Revelation 8:5 has this same exact theophany, which is considered the first since it is the first time in Revelation it occurred. Luke 17:24 says, "For as the lightning flashes and lights up the sky from one side to the other, so will the Son of Man be in his day." Lightning is the method for each rapture group to meet Jesus in the sky. This is the same method it was for Elijah in 2 Kings 2:11 where "chariots of fire" is considered a metaphor to lightning.

> Then God's temple in heaven was opened, and the ark of his covenant was seen within his temple. There were *flashes of lightning, rumblings, peals of thunder, an earthquake, and heavy hail.* (Rev. 11:19, emphasis to second great eschatological theophany)

SECOND – MESSENGERS WILL PURIFY THE JEWISH PEOPLE

Malachi 3:1–5 says that the Lord is sending a messenger who will prepare the way before him and purify the Jewish people. Malachi 3:6 follows that the Lord will draw near to you for judgment. Zechariah 13:7–9 says that the Jewish people will be refined and two-thirds of them will be struck down. Since the witnesses are here to purify the Jewish people, it is reasonable that they would be here when the Antichrist is persecuting them, which is expected during the majority, if not all, of the second half of the seventieth week of Daniel.

Malachi 3:1 has a near far prophecy. It was first fulfilled with John the Baptist, who was a form of Elijah, in Matthew 17:12–13. "But I tell you that Elijah has already come . . . Then the disciples understood that he was speaking to them of John the Baptist." The second fulfillment is eschatological, when the two witnesses arrive several days before Jesus's return on Day 1. This same Day 1 is when the Jerusalem battle counter attack by Jesus against the Antichrist coalition begins.

> Behold, I am sending My messenger (*Elijah*), and he will clear a way before Me (Jesus's arrival *on Day 1*). And the Lord, whom you are seeking, will suddenly come to His temple; and the messenger of the covenant, in whom you delight, behold, He is coming," says the LORD of armies. "But who can endure the day of His coming? (*first eschatological Day of the Lord*) And who can stand when He appears? For He is like a refiner's fire, and like launderer's soap. And He will sit as a smelter and purifier of silver, and He will purify the sons of Levi and refine them like gold and silver, so that they may present to the LORD offerings in righteousness. (Mal. 3:1–3 NASB, emphasis added)

THIRD – GENTILES TRAMPLE JERUSALEM FORTY-TWO MONTHS AND WITNESSES PROPHECY 1,260 DAYS

Most scholars have the great tribulation in Matthew 24:21 starting on Day 1 identified with the abomination from Daniel 9:27 and Matthew 24:15. This same duration (second half of the seventieth week) and context (abomination) can be found in Revelation 11:2–3. These Scriptures provide support that the Antichrist and the two witnesses time on earth will overlap quite a bit.

> [B]ut do not measure the court outside the temple; leave that out, for it is given over to the nations, and they will trample the holy city for forty-two months. And I will grant authority to my two witnesses, and they will prophesy for 1,260 days, clothed in sackcloth. (Rev. 11:2–3)

FOURTH – WITNESSES ON EARTH FOR 1,263.5 DAYS PLUS

In Revelation 11:3 the two witnesses will prophecy for 1,260 days. In Revelation 11:7–9 the two witnesses will be killed and dead for three and a half days. "But after the three and a half days a breath of life from God entered them, and they stood up on their feet, and great fear fell on those who saw them. Then they heard a loud voice from heaven saying to them, "Come up here!" And they went up to heaven in a cloud, and their enemies watched them." (Rev. 11:11–12). So, they were on earth for 1,260 days, then killed and left in the street three and a half days dead before being raised back to life for some unknown amount of time and then returning to heaven.

Consider the Bible says the two witnesses were dead for three and a half days. However, it is silent on how long they remained on earth before being called to heaven. It is not reasonable after coming back to life that they were on earth for anything close to the three and a half days. This duration relative to three and a half days must be much less. Or else, why would the Bible not say how long? Therefore, this much less duration is considered likely between a fraction of a day up to about one literal day. This will later be supported as one half a day.

FIFTH – ISRAEL RAPTURED ON DAY 1,260

The Israel rapture of Revelation 11:19 has the same theophany language — "peals of thunder, rumblings, flashes of lightning, and an earthquake" — as Revelation 8:5, which occurred on a one-day event. This indicates that Israel will be physically saved in the later seventh blown trumpet of Revelation 11:19 with the same exact theophany. This theophany includes the *lightning flashes* of Luke 17:24 with the return of the Son of Man. Just as the first great eschatological theophany was a one-day event, the second eschatological theophany is proposed to also be a one-day event. Later in chapter 11 (Ten Days of Awe), the sixth blown trumpet is proposed to likely be nine days. Since this theory is based on Yom Kippur being on Day 1,260, it is reasonable that Scripture is pointing to a tenth day for the seventh blown trumpet, i.e., a one-day event.

Sometime during the three and a half days in Revelation 11:10, gifts are being exchanged since the witnesses are dead. Those exchanged gifts are likely from those with the mark of the beast and who worship his image. Afterward the witnesses come back to life they are called up to heaven. Then in v. 13 there was an earthquake, and they were "terrified and gave glory to the God of heaven," though there is no reference to them repenting of their sins. Verses 12–13 are the end of the sixth blown trumpet.

WITNESSES – FIVE-DAY TIMELINE

From figure 10 we saw the prevalent differences of five and seven days from 2023 to 2040. A timeline of these two prevalent differences is conceptually shown in figures 11 and 12.

These two figures were conceptualized with the witnesses being alive for half a day after being dead for three and a half days. Within each figure the "W" abbreviation is followed by a number representing how many literal days the two witnesses had been on earth. There are two six-day (W1 to W7) differences in 2042 (4 to 10 April 2042) and 2049 (16 to 22 April 2049) which do not work since Israel would be too old by 2034 as discussed in chapter 9. The five-day (W1 to W6) timeline is a much stronger chronological position than the seven-day (W1 to W8) timeline for the following reasons.

First, if seven days is used, then figure 12 points to no scriptural events on Days 1,258 and 1,259.

Second, figure 16 in chapter 11 points to a five–day (W1 to W6) witness timeline having a *perfect* fit for the ten Days of Awe (Day 1,251 to 1,260).

FIGURE 11: TWO WITNESSES FIVE-DAY (W1 TO W6) TIMELINE (GREAT FIT)

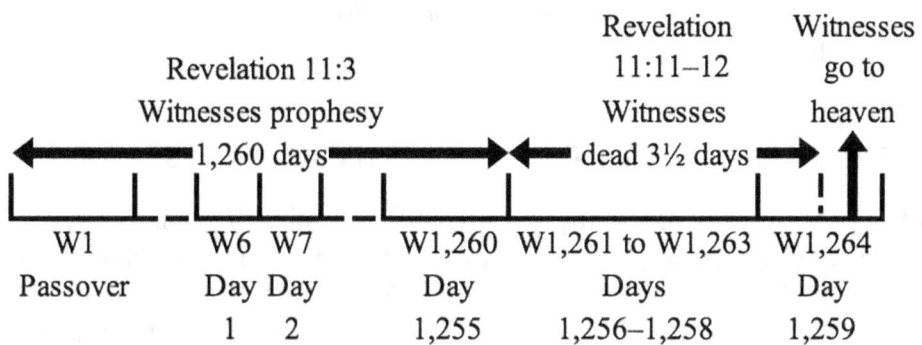

FIGURE 12: TWO WITNESSES SEVEN-DAY (W1 TO W8) TIMELINE (POOR FIT)

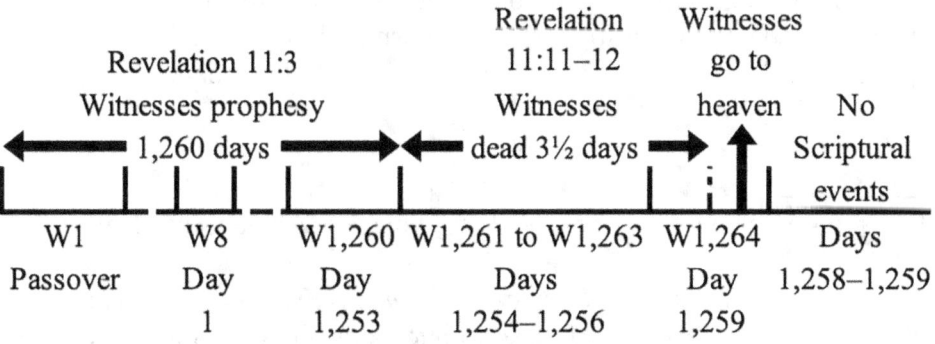

PASSOVER ESCHATOLOGICAL MEANING

The Passover having an eschatological meaning of the Messiah's arrival to earth, possibly foreshadowing *the initial* arrival, is supported by Travis M. Snow in *The Passover King Exploring the Prophetic Connection between Passover, the End Times, and the Return of Jesus*.[1] Emphasis added in the quote is by Travis Snow.

> My primary intention is simply to highlight that in addition to the words of Jesus in Luke 22:15–16, we also have testimony from other Jewish sages who lived in the first century, which indicates that they too understood Passover to have an eschatological significance that is linked to the establishment of God's kingdom. . . . This text shows us that there was actually a broader debate in Judaism in the first century over which Biblical holiday most clearly foreshadows *the initial* arrival of the Messiah to this earth.

WITNESSES ARRIVE AT A FUTURE FAMILY'S PASSOVER

Imagine a Jewish family living in Jerusalem celebrating their annual Passover with the Seder dinner set. Then after the third cup is drunk, which is the cup of blessing (1 Cor. 10:16), a family member walks to their outside door as by Jewish custom to see if Elijah is there.[2] Before the family member, usually a child, arrives to the door, there is a knock. Opening the door, there is a man dressed in a coarse, dark, woven material of either camel or goat hair (sackcloth) with a leather belt around his waist. After the parents talk with him at the doorstep, they learn he is Elijah (or perhaps the second witness), and then the family invites him in for a meal, which the family already has an empty Seder place setting for! The Jewish tradition of having Elijah visit appears a real possibility for two Jewish families in Jerusalem on a Sabbath.

---

1 Travis M. Snow, *The Passover King*, Voice of Messiah, Inc., Dallas, TX, © 2020, 15.
2 Alfred Edersheim, *The Temple – Its Ministry and Services As They Were at the Time of Jesus Christ*, Kregel Publications, Grand Rapids, MI 49501, © 1997, 153.

Filter #2, Two Witnesses Arrive on a Passover

Imagine the discussion that night and the next morning when the family is contacting all their family and friends and then fleeing Jerusalem. They could be directed to wait for the abomination of destruction on Day 1 and then position themselves on the east side of the temple mount to escape the Antichrist persecution for 1,260 days. What a blessing to have advance notice of how to prepare!

SOME FEASTS OF THE LORD SOURCES ARE INCORRECT

This was the most challenging chapter to write. One of the challenges was that there were different sources I was using for Passover and Yom Kippur. Two sources incorrectly had the beginning of the Passover on the next day.[3] Using an incorrect one-day later Passover date was causing my calendar math for the witnesses to leave on Day 1,260 in the seventh blown trumpet verses the sixth blown trumpet on Day 1,259 in Revelation 11:12–15. Fortunately, further study revealed the correct Passover annual dates. If I had not discovered these two data source calendar errors, I would have never written this chapter. Since chapter 11 (Ten Days of Awe) leverages this chapter, it would also not of been written.

CONCLUSION

This chapter examined the years from 2023 to 2050 and 2067 with a subset shown in figure 10 comparing the annual Passover to when the witnesses might arrive. Their arrival date is based on 1,264 days before Day 1,259. This is where Day 1,259 was proposed as the day when they were called up to heaven and also being the last day of the sixth blown trumpet. The best fit conceptual figure 11 timeline was based on them arriving five days before Day 1 on a Passover.

This 1,264-day conceptual timeline figure 11 is based on five days (W1 to W6), which provides a strong case that the two witnesses will arrive on a Passover as Jewish tradition expects. The end of this same conceptual timeline is also supported since the witnesses appear from Scripture to

---

3 Hebcal.com, "Jewish Holidays 2022–2023", accessed March 28, 2021, https://www.hebcal.com/holidays/2022–2023 and M. Greenfield, *150 Year Calendar with corresponding English and Hebrew dates including Holidays, Sidras and Haftoras*, © 1963.

leave earth on the last day of the sixth blown trumpet. This day is supported as Day 1,259.

This is supported with the seventh blown trumpet being a one-day event on Day 1,260. The Beyond Prewrath eschatological position has a rapture of the elect in Revelation 8:5 and of Israel in Revelation 11:19. Both great theophanies are exactly the same. Since the first is a one-day event, the second rapture for Israel is also proposed to be a one-day event.

Witnesses leaving earth on Day 1,257 for the seven-day timeline was shown much less favorable since that would mean Days 1,258 and 1,259 would seem to have no scriptural events happening then. Other supporting reasons were provided.

Chapter 8

Filter #3, 75 Days

The idea for this filter began when I considered the *The Sign of Christ's Coming and End of the Age* by Robert van Kampen with its 75 days from Yom Kippur to Hanukkah.[1] Kevin Howard and Marvin Rosenthal *The Feasts of the Lord God's Prophetic Calendar from Calvary to the Kingdom* discuss Hanukkah also as being 75 days after Yom Kippur.[2] Consider the importance of this since Jesus was in the temple during Hanukkah in John 10:22–23. These eschatological 75 days are divided into a 30-day segment (Days 1,261 to 1,290) followed by 45-day segment (Days 1,291 to 1,335) as shown in figure 14.

> At that time the Feast of Dedication (Hanukkah) took place at Jerusalem. It was winter, and Jesus was walking in the temple, in the colonnade of Solomon. (John 10:22–23)

My thought was to examine the differences in duration between these annual holidays to see if it was always 75 days as one would expect. Note that the Hebrew month of Chislev in Nehemiah 1:1 and Zechariah 7:1 was later renamed as Kislev. When I made a spreadsheet of the various years in figure 13, I found to my surprise that there are many years where the difference was 74 days! I do not know why the Hebrew calendar is this way. Since prophecy requires 75 days, those years with a 74 day difference cannot fulfill prophecy.

---

1 Robert Van Kampen, *The Sign of Christ's Coming and the End of the Age*, Published by Crossway Books, a publishing ministry of Good News Publishers, 1300 Crescent Street, Wheaton, Illinois 60187, 1992, 482.

2 Kevin Howard and Marvin Rosenthal, *The Feasts of the Lord God's Prophetic Calendar from Calvary to the Kingdom*, Published in Nashville, Tennessee, by Thomas Nelson, Inc., 1997, 159–160.

FIGURE 13: YOM KIPPUR TO HANNUKAH – 75 DAYS

Year	Yom Kippur Tishri 10	Hanukkah Kislev 25	Difference in days
2026	20 Sep.	4 Dec.	75
2027	10 Oct.	24 Dec.	75
2028	29 Sep.	12 Dec.	74
2029	18 Sep.	1 Dec.	74
2030	6 Oct.	20 Dec.	75
2031	26 Sep.	9 Dec.	74
2032	14 Sep.	27 Nov.	74
2033	2 Oct.	16 Dec.	75
2034	22 Sep.	6 Dec.	75
2070	15 Sep.	28 Nov.	74

Robert van Kampen in *The Sign of Christ's Coming and End of the Age* called this 30-day segment the reclamation period followed by the 45-day segment as the restoration period.

1) The *reclamation period* is when the last of God's wrath of seven bowls are poured out. This 30-day segment begins on Day 1,261 and ends on Day 1,290 as derived from Daniel 9:27, 12:11–12, and Revelation 11:19.

2) The *restoration period* of 45 days begins on Day 1,291 and ends on Day 1,335 (Dan. 12:12). In Isaiah 24:1 we see during the restoration period. "Behold, the LORD will empty the earth and make it desolate, and he will twist its surface and scatter its inhabitants."

Hanukkah was first celebrated as a rededication of the second temple.[3] Hanukkah (Day 1,335) is expected at the start of the new millennium so would be celebrated 75 days following the last Day of Atonement (Yom Kippur) on Day 1,260. Christ's physical, one thousand-year rule over the

---

3 Sam Nadler, *Messiah in The Feasts of Israel*, Word of Messiah Ministries, Charlotte, NC, 178.

earth would begin on Day 1,335.[4] Yom Kippur is also when the glory of Christ returns to the temple.[5]

FIGURE 14: 30- AND 45-DAY SEGMENTS

End of trumpets	End of bowls	Start of millennium	End of millennium
Seven bowls 30 days Day 1261–1290 Dan. 12:11–12	Earth restored 45 days Day 1291–1335 Dan. 12:11–12	Old earth with "twisted crust" Isa. 65:18–25 Rev. 20:1–6	New earth Isa. 65:17 Rev. 21
Day 1260 Old earth	Day 1290 Earth's crust "twisted" Isa. 24:1 Rev. 16:20	Day 1335 First population event	Great white throne Second population event

[F]rom the time that the regular burnt offering is taken away and the abomination that makes desolate is set up, there shall be 1,290 days. Blessed is he who waits and arrives at the 1,335 days. (Dan. 12:11–12)

[J]udas and his brethren with the whole congregation of Israel ordained, that the days of the dedication of the altar should be kept in their season from year to year by the space of eight days, from the five and twentieth day of the month Chislev, with mirth and gladness. (1 Macc. 4:59 KJV 1611)

---

4 Robert Van Kampen, *The Sign of Christ's Coming and the End of the Age*, Published by Crossway Books, a publishing ministry of Good News Publishers, 1300 Crescent Street, Wheaton, Illinois 60187, 1992, 475.
5 Ibid.

CONCLUSION

Day 1,260 is representative of the end of seventieth week of Daniel. If Day 1,335 is representative of the start of millennium, then there should be a difference of 75 days, though figure 13 shows that some years have a difference of 74 days. This assumes the seven poured bowls are after the seventieth week of Daniel. Those years with a difference of 74 days would not fulfill future prophetic Scripture and, therefore, must be excluded as possible candidates for an Israel rapture on Day 1,260 in Revelation 11:19.

Chapter 9

This Generation

PREMISE

The premise of this chapter is that the Olivet Discourse of Matthew 24:1–2 has been prophetically fulfilled in 70 AD, though the balance of the Olivet Discourse from Matthew 24:3 to 25:46 has not been fulfilled. Matthew 24:34 has this generation to not pass away until the prophecy is fulfilled. Since Matthew 24:3ff has not been fulfilled, it points to a future Israel generation. This future next generation will be called the second generation.

THIS (FIRST) GENERATION: WHO?

The Siege of Jerusalem in the year 70 CE was the decisive event of the First Jewish-Roman War, in which the Roman general Titus' army captured the city of Jerusalem and destroyed both the city and its temple.[1] The siege of the city began on 14 April 70 CE, three days before the Passover that year.[2] Many of the casualties were religious Jews from across their world such as from Babylon and Egypt wanting to celebrate the yearly Passover in Jerusalem but instead got trapped in the chaotic siege.[3] These Jews were the prophetic first generation.

---

1 Josephus *The Complete Works* translated by William Whiston A.M., *The War of the Jews*, Book 3, Chapters 1 to 4.
2 Schäfer, Peter (2003), *The History of the Jews in the Greco–Roman World: The Jews of Palestine from Alexander the Great to the Arab*, Conquest Routledge, 129–130; *War of the Jews Book V*, sect. 99 (Ch. 3, paragraph 1 in Whiston's translation); dates given are approximations since the correspondence between the calendar Josephus used and modern calendars is uncertain.
3 Josephus, BJ, 6.9.3., Perseus Project BJ6.9.3.

THIS (FIRST) GENERATION: START DATE

The first generation start date is when Jesus gave his prophecy in Matthew 24:1–2 on the Mount of Olives several days before his crucifixion. This was discussed in chapter 6 as 26 to 36 AD.

THIS (FIRST) GENERATION: END DATE

Matthew 24:1–2 prophecy of no stone being upon another was fulfilled in 70 AD when the temple was destroyed as described by the historian Flavius Josephus.[4] What occurred was a fulfillment of Leviticus 26:33 prophecy of their future disobedience, and, therefore, they would be scattered among the nations and their land becoming desolate. 70 AD became the end date of the first generation.

> And I will scatter you among the nations, and I will unsheathe the sword after you, and your land shall be a desolation, and your cities shall be a waste. (Lev. 26:33)

> But he answered them, "You see all these, do you not? Truly, I say to you, there will not be left here one stone upon another that will not be thrown down." (Matt. 24:2)

> "... This (western) wall was spared, in order to afford a camp for such as were to lie in garrison; as were the towers also spared, ... but for all the rest of the wall, it was so thoroughly laid even with the ground by those that dug it up to the foundation, that there was left nothing to make those that came thither believe it had ever been inhabited. ..." (Flavius Josephus)

THIS (FIRST) GENERATION: LIFE EXPECTANCY

Who was this first-generation Jesus referring to? It was the Jewish people whom the apostles were told to witness and heal. So, what was their life expectancy later when the prophecy was fulfilled in 70 AD?

Population Council, Estimates of Regional and Global Expectancy, 1800–2001 by James C. Riley says, "Global life expectancy at birth was

---

[4] Josephus *The Complete Works* translated by William Whiston A.M., *The War of the Jews, Book 7, Chapter 1.*

about 28.5 years in 1800."[5] Samuel H. Preston *"Human Mortality throughout History and Prehistory"* has global life expectancy as between 20 and 30 years before 1600.[6] The Israel life-span will be shown in the following paragraphs to be much longer than this historic norm of that era.

During Jesus's ministry he healed multitudes of people and raised many from the dead (Matt. 15:30–31). In Matthew 15:24 it says, "I (Jesus) was sent only to the lost sheep of the house of Israel." Of course, we know the Gentiles are grafted in, according to Ephesians 3:6 which says, "This mystery is that the Gentiles are fellow heirs, members of the same body, and partakers of the promise in Christ Jesus through the gospel."

Healing authority was given by Jesus to his twelve disciples in Matthew 10:1–8 who were directed to only go to Israel and not the Gentiles or Samaritans. When Jesus died on the cross, "The tombs also were opened." Matthew 27:52–53 continues "And many bodies of the saints who had fallen asleep were raised, and coming out the tombs after his resurrection they went into the holy city and appeared to many." From Matthew 19:13 we also know Jesus rebuked the disciples such that little children would not be hindered to come to him and that Jesus placed his hands on them and prayed. In Acts 5:12–16 we see *multitudes* of people being healed of sickness by the apostles. Healing of the sick was so pronounced that in Acts 5:14–16 that they carried the sick into the streets and laid them on cots and mats so that as Peter walked by, his shadow might fall on some and heal them. Scripture says in v. 16 that *all* were healed, not a few or many.

> And more than ever believers were added to the Lord, multitudes of both men and women, so that they even carried out the sick into the streets and laid them on cots and mats, that as Peter came by at least his shadow might fall on some of them. The people also gathered from the towns around Jerusalem, bringing the sick and those afflicted with unclean spirits, and they were all healed. (Acts 5:14–16)

---

5 Population Council, Estimates of Reginal and Global Life Expectancy, 1800 2001, James C. Riley, 537, accessed March 28, 2021, https://u.demog.berkeley.edu/~jrw/Biblio/Eprints/%20P-S/riley.2005_estimates.global.e0.pdf (berkeley.edu).

6 Samuel H. Preston, 1996, *Human Mortality throughout History and Prehistory*. In Julian L. Simon (ed.), *The State of Humanity*, Boston: Blackwell, 30.

This describes wide spread healing in Israel for the Jews! Young women, as Jesus and the apostles touched their bodies, would have been healed. Any unseen issues with women's future wombs for birth would be healed. Later births would, therefore, have a low infant mortality rate, if any. Therefore, the life expectancy in Israel realistically could have been raised by at least a decade or more by 70 AD.

From Jesus Olivet prophecy, it would require this first-generation life expectancy in 70 AD as thirty-four to forty-three years, which is reflective of Pilates ten-year reign from 26 AD to 36 AD.[7] This first lifespan definition then becomes the definition of the second lifespan generation. The first does not have the same length as the second since the current Israel lifespan is significantly longer than in 70 AD.

Many Jews were aware of the Olivet prophecy that the temple would be destroyed in their first generation, so they started leaving Jerusalem a few years in advance of 70 AD. The Jewish revolt against the Romans in 66 AD also provided guidance to the lead up to the destruction of Jerusalem. What a blessing to know prophecy from Jesus and leave prior to Jerusalem being attacked.

THE GREAT DIASPORA

The great diaspora began in 70 AD with the destruction of the second temple. It ended on 14 May 1948 when Israel became a sovereign nation again. There have been several earlier Jewish diasporas, such as Egyptian for about four hundred years, Assyrian for about two hundred years, and Babylonian for 70 years. Yet, there is still one more diaspora coming to Israel starting on Day 1. Jewish exiles will be persecuted (Dan. 9:27; Zech. 13:7–9; 14:5; c.f. Matt. 24:15–21), though a separate Jewish remnant will be protected for 1,260 days (Rev. 12:6–17).

THIS (SECOND) GENERATION – START DATE

Since the 70 AD diaspora, there have only been two significant Jewish land acquired events. The first was on 14 May 1948 when Israel became a nation again with the scattered Jewish people returning to their homeland. This was a significant prophetic event, which was fulfilled with Ezekiel 11:17 and

---

7 Harold W. Hoehner, *Chronological Aspects of the Life of Christ*, 1973, 98.

Deuteronomy 30:5. A second possible generation start date could be when Israel took control of the Jerusalem temple mount in 1967. It is unclear from Scripture whether the second generational start date began on 1948 or 1967, so both will be examined.

> Therefore say, 'Thus says the Lord GOD: I will gather you from the peoples and assemble you out of the countries where you have been scattered, and I will give you the land of Israel.' (Ezek. 11:17)

> And the LORD your God will bring you into the land that your fathers possessed, that you may possess it. And he will make you more prosperous and numerous than your fathers. (Deut. 30:5)

THIS (SECOND) GENERATION – TEMPLE MOUNT

Daniel 9:27 prophecy requires the temple abomination of desolation to occur on Day 1. Jesus prophesied this same abomination in Matthew 24:15, which is parallel to the fifth open seal in Revelation 6:9–11. This means that prior to the abomination a temple must be built.

The 1948 and 1967 events assure us that Israel is in a position to build a temple. The temple only needs adequate size and configuration for the priests to perform their daily duties, which include sacrifices in the evening and morning. If the temple being described in Ezekiel 40–41 and Revelation 11:1 is this third temple, then it may be grandeur in structure.

THIS (SECOND) GENERATION – LENGTH?

The second generation of the Jewish people appears to end when they are physically raptured on Day 1,260 in Revelation 11:19. As of 2017, the Organization for Economic Co–Operation and Development has the average Israel life expectancy as 82.6 years.[8] Over the last several decades, the life expectancy growth rate has slowed in Israel and the world. It may be possible to add another two or three years in Israel by about 2030 if an advancement

---

8 Organization for Economic Co–Operation and Development (OECD) 2017 Israel life expectancy of 82.6, accessed March 28, 2021, https://stats.oecd.org/index.aspx?queryid=30114.

is made in health care. Assuming this best-case, lifespan increase scenario, three years will be added to make the second-generation length 85.6 years.

CONCLUSION

If the second-generation prophetic lifespan began on 14 May 1948 and the current life expectancy in Israel is 82.6 years, then we could expect the end of the seventieth week of Daniel to occur before the end of the year 2030. If their lifespan is extended with medical advancements by three years, then Day 1,260 would occur before the end of 2033.

Chapter 10

Show a Blessing to Pregnant and Nursing Women

The feasts of the Lord theory proposes[1] that the second fall feast Yom Kippur is at the end of the seventieth week of Daniel called Day 1,260. During the middle of this seventieth week in Daniel 9:27 is when the abomination of desolation in the Jerusalem temple will occur.

> And he shall make a strong covenant with many for one week, and for half of the week (Day 1) he shall put an end to sacrifice and offering. And on the wing of abominations shall come one who makes desolate, until the decreed end is poured out on the desolator. (Dan. 9:27)

Yom Kippur annual dates from 2023 to 2050 were examined, which all ranged Day 1 (three and a half years earlier) from 4 April to 2 May. Figure 15 shows a select sample of these Day 1 dates from the years 2023 to 2031 and on 2067. None of these Day 1 dates occur on a Sabbath or in the winter, which will be a dual future blessing!

The first blessing is since their day of escape from the Antichrist and ten kings is not on a Jewish Sabbath. The Sabbath would limit their travel to a short distance. Acts 1:12 defined a Sabbath day's distance from Jerusalem to the Mount of Olives, which is approximately two-thirds of a mile. This distance would not be enough to separate them from the Jerusalem holocaust. Zechariah 13:7–9 describes this holocaust in Israel. This holocaust begins five days after the Passover, so there would be expected many Jews in Jerusalem with the likely new temple celebration.[2]

> And alas for women who are pregnant and for those who are nursing infants in those days! Pray that your flight may not be in winter or on a Sabbath. (Matt. 24:19–20)

---

1 See chapter 1, note 12.
2 See chapter 7 which has the two witnesses arriving five days before Day 1 on a Passover.

Then they returned to Jerusalem from the mount called Olivet, which is near Jerusalem, a Sabbath day's journey away. (Acts 1:12)

FIGURE 15: DAY 1 DATES – ALL IN SPRING AND NOT ON A SABBATH

Day 1 (1,259 days before Yom Kippur)	Yom Kippur (Day 1,260)
Monday, April 10, 2023 (Spring)	20 Sep. 2026
Monday, April 29, 2024 (Spring)	10 Oct. 2027
Saturday, April 19, 2025 (Spring)	29 Sep. 2028
Wednesday, April 8, 2026 (Spring)	18 Sep. 2029
Monday, April 26, 2027 (Spring)	6 Oct. 2030
Saturday, April 15, 2028 (Spring)	26 Sep. 2031
Wednesday, April 4, 2029 (Spring)	14 Sep. 2032
Monday, April 22, 2030 (Spring)	2 Oct. 2033
Saturday, April 12, 2031 (Spring)	22 Sep. 2034
Tuesday, April 5, 2067 (Spring)	15 Sep. 2070

JEWS IN JERUSALEM ESCAPE BY WATER

Jesus warns in Matthew 24:16 that when the abomination of desolation comes "then let those who are in Judea flee to the mountains." Zechariah 14:4–5 parallel directs those in Jerusalem to flee to the mountain valley just created to the east. It seems on that Day 1, if not shortly before, "Living waters shall flow out from Jerusalem, half of them to the eastern sea and half of them to the western sea. It shall continue in summer as in winter" (Zech. 14:8). Isaiah 33:21 has broad rivers and streams with a depth that no oars can go. This living water which begins flowing could also be representative of Ezekiel 47:1–6.

> On that day His feet (Jesus) will stand on the Mount of Olives, which is in front of Jerusalem on the east; and the Mount of Olives will be split in its middle from east to west forming a very large valley. Half of the mountain will move toward the north, and the other half toward the south. And you will flee by the valley of My mountains, for the valley of the mountains will reach to Azel (likely Jordanian mountains); yes, you will flee just as you fled from the earthquake in the days of Uzziah king of Judah. Then the Lord, my God, will come, and all the holy ones with Him! (Zech. 14:4–5 NASB)

Could the means of escape for those Jews living in Jerusalem be as simple as jumping into a river just created by the Lord? This is a real possibility. Average air temperatures for the months January to March are 46°F, 48°F and 53°F, respectively.[3] Winter cold-water temperatures could cause hypothermia if exposed for an extended duration, especially for the wombs of women with unborn children. Warmer spring weather water temperatures are ideal. These reasons could be why it would be a blessing to not happen in the colder winter months.

> On that day there will be no light; the luminaries will die out. For it will be a unique day which is known to the LORD, neither day nor night, but it will come about that at the time of evening there will be light. And on that day living waters will flow out of Jerusalem, half of them toward the eastern sea and the other half toward the western sea; it will be in summer as well as in winter. (Zech. 14:6–8 NASB)

There are two other blessings, though not explicitly stated in Scripture. First, in Zechariah 14:6–8 lack of light could provide concealment for those escaping. Second, the mountains moving and forming a valley to the east could disrupt an attacking force in that direction. The enemy's own survival of escaping a mountain collapsing followed by a flood of water would become their greater priority. In fact, "The whole land shall be turned into a plain from Geba to Rimmon south of Jerusalem. But Jerusalem shall remain aloft . . ." (Zech. 14:10).

---

3 Holiday–Weather.com, https://www.holiday-weather.com/jerusalem/averages/.

Jerusalem is the epicenter of the Antichrist persecution, though consider that those Jews who escape to the east are the only ones on earth who are promised protection from persecution for 1,260 days in Revelation 12:13–14. Jews who jump in the river flowing toward the western sea of the Mediterranean are not Scripturally promised the Lord's protection.

If you are not a Jew, don't position yourself on the east side of the temple mount to escape the great tribulation with the Jewish remnant of Revelation 12:13–16. As a Gentile, you are not promised protection of escape, and to make your situation worse, you would be at the epicenter of the Antichrist's wrath. Gentiles should stay as far away as possible!

CONCLUSION

If this understanding of Scripture is correct, then there would be a fulfilled scriptural blessing to pregnant and nursing women since Day 1 is not in the winter or on a Sabbath. The blessing of the event not occurring in the winter could be because their only means of escaping the Antichrist's persecution could be by jumping into the water when the water temperature is moderate in the spring. Also, having a partial day of no sunlight in Zechariah 14:6–7 would prevent any sun exposure to the skin. The event not occurring during the Sabbath would not limit their escape distance.

Chapter 12 overview in figure 19 has the most probable Day 1 dates as 26 April 2027 or 22 April 2030. Both of these days start four days before their Sabbath. Having four days to escape before their Sabbath would provide an even greater blessing. If 7 June 1967 is used as a start date, then 5 to 6 April 2067 in figure 20 would be Day 1.

Chapter 11

Ten Days of Awe

PURPOSE

To propose the last ten days within the seventieth week of Daniel has an eschatological meaning of the Days of Awe. The Days of Awe become the sixth and seventh blown trumpets. Since the last day of these Days of Awe is Day 1,260 then the earlier Feast of Trumpets is on Day 1,251. The four angels arriving incrementally from the temple in Revelation 14:14–18 and the "clean up" in Revelation 14:20 will incrementally be shown to represent Days 1,251 to 1,255. All angels leave the temple or altar separately, though arrive in time for the Jehoshaphat battle described in more detail in Revelation 9:13–21.

Days 1,256 to 1,259 form the last four days of the sixth blown trumpet. Three and a half days are associated with the death of the two witnesses (Rev. 11:7–11) and a half day deduced as when they are taken to heaven on Day 1,259. Chapter 7 helps support this position.

Day 1,260 is the rapture of Israel in Revelation 11:19 in the seventh blown trumpet, just as the rapture of the elect in Revelation 8:5 was on one day.

DAY 1251 – JEWISH NEW YEAR

The Jewish civil New Year begins on Rosh Hashanah (Feasts of Trumpets). This is when their calendar is increased by one year. Figure 16 identifies this day as Day 1,251, which is nine days before the Yom Kippur on Day 1,260.

FIGURE 16: TEN DAYS OF AWE

←——————— Ten Days of Awe ———————→									
←——————— Sixth trumpet (T) ———————→									T #7 →
Light	Darkness		Light		Light				
Rev. 14:14-20 Harvest of Wicked					Rev. 11: 7-11				
v14	vv15-16	v17	vv18-19	v20					
No work	Reap #1	No work	Reap #2	Clean up	Witnesses dead 3.5 days			Rev. 11:12	Rev. 11 vv15-19
Day 1251	Day 1252	Day 1253	Day 1254	Day 1255	Day 1256	Day 1257	Day 1258	Day 1259	Day 1260
Feast of Trumpets (New Year)			↑ Joel 3:1-2; 9-16 Rev. 9:13-21 Horsemen Jehoshaphat Campaign						Yom Kippur Rev. 15

DAYS 1,251 TO 1,255 – THE REAPERS – TIME SPACING IN DAYS

In Revelation 14:15–18 each angel came individually out from the temple in heaven then traveled toward earth. This indicates there was some amount of time spacing between each angel. Otherwise, why would an angel not wait a few moments for another angel to join him for the journey to earth from the temple or altar area?

Consider the hypothesis that each of these five separate events in Revelation 14:14–20 is one day long. Then Revelation 14:14 would be Day 1,251 when Christ sat on a cloud not doing any work. The next paragraph examines if any work was done during a Sabbath.

WORK DAYS – DAYS 1,252; 1,254; AND 1,255

The three work days of 1,252, 1,254, and 1,255 will be examined whether they occur on a Sabbath, which starts on Friday night. If any of these work days do, then we need to provide a fourth filter as not viable return dates of Christ.

Christ began to reap in Revelation 14:16 after the first messenger angel arrived from the temple in Revelation 14:15, which is shown in figure 17 as Day 1,252. Figure 17 calendar dates are based from year Yom Kippur being Day 1,260. None of the figure 17 dates are on a Sabbath except for the first row for reap #1 on 12 September 2026. This would equate to the seventieth week of Daniel starting in 2020, which has already passed. Therefore, a fourth filter is not needed in this analysis.

The last two columns of figure 17 are for Day 1,254 (reap #2) and 1,255 (clean-up). None of these other dates are on a Sabbath. Since there is no work on the Sabbath then Chapter 12 has no prophecy date restrictions. Matthew 13:39 identifies these days as the end of the age with the angels reaping the weeds sown by the devil. Figure 17 dates are representative of 14 May 1948, except the last row for 7 June 1967.

> The field is the world, and the good seed is the sons of the kingdom. The weeds are the sons of the evil one, and the enemy who sowed them is the devil. The harvest is the end of the age, and the reapers are angels. (Matt. 13:38–39)

FIGURE 17: WORK DAYS FOR 1,252, 1,254, AND 1,255

Yom Kippur Day 1,260	Reap #1, Day 1,252	Reap #2, Day 1,254	Clean–up, Day 1,255
20 Sep. 2026	*Fri., 12 Sep.*	Mon., 14 Sep.	Tue., 15 Sep.
10 Oct. 2027	Sat., 2 Oct.	Mon., 4 Oct.	Tue., 5 Oct.
29 Sep. 2028	Thu., 21 Sep.	Sat., 23 Sep.	Sun., 24 Sep.
18 Sep. 2029	Mon., 10 Sep.	Wed., 12 Sep.	Thu., 13 Sep.
6 Oct. 2030	Sat., 28 Sep.	Mon., 30 Sep.	Tue., 1 Oct.
26 Sep. 2031	Thu., 18 Sep.	Sat., 20 Sep.	Sun., 21 Sep.
14 Sep. 2032	Mon., 6 Sep.	Wed., 8 Sep.	Thu., 9 Sep.
2 Oct. 2033	Sat., 24 Sep.	Mon., 26 Sep.	Tue., 27 Sep.
22 Sep. 2034	Thu., 14 Sep.	Sat., 16 Sep.	Sun., 17 Sep.
12 Oct. 2035	Thu., 4 Oct.	Sat., 6 Oct.	Sun., 7 Oct.
30 Sep. 2036	Mon., 22 Sep.	Wed., 24 Sep.	Thu., 25 Sep.
15 Sep. 2070	Sun., 7 Sep.	Tue., 9 Sep.	Wed., 10 Sep.

IS HEAVEN WITHIN A SABBATH DAY'S JOURNEY?

If Day 1,251 was a Sabbath day (as in 1 October 2027, 27 September 2030, and 23 September 2033) and Jesus arrived at that time, as described in the previous paragraph, then it is interesting to note that heaven would be within a Sabbath day's journey. These first two dates are the most probable dates of his return as shown later in figure 19. This Sabbath day earthly distance is defined from Acts 1:12 as the distance from Jerusalem to the Mount of Olives.

Perhaps the universal (heaven and earth) measurement of a Sabbath day's journey might be the equivalent of travel time duration rather than distance? The time to travel by foot between the temple and the Mount of Olives using the eastern temple gate is about 20 to 30 minutes. The distance is just under a mile though the terrain is mountainous. So, could it be that heaven is within 30 minutes of earth, though time dilation would extend the distance significantly? Chapter 3 of *Beyond Prewrath End–Time Prophecy* discusses this further.

Ten Days of Awe 63

DAYS 1251 TO 1255 – HARVEST OF THE WICKED – FIVE SEPARATE EVENTS

Revelation 14:14–20 harvest of the earth seven verses appears to have five separate events, separated by angels coming out of the temple or altar area, and then the clean-up in Revelation 14:20 after the Revelation 14:18–19 battle. Since the earthly temple is occupied by the Gentiles (Rev. 11:2), we have to assume the angels are coming from a heavenly temple. The five separate Scriptural events are:

> [B]ut do not measure the court outside the temple; leave that out, for it is given over to the nations, and they will trample the holy city for forty-two months. (Rev. 11:2)

1) *Revelation 14:14, No work*: In Revelation 14:14 Christ is sitting on a white cloud with a sharp sickle. No work appears to occur. No reference to darkness.

2) *Revelation 14:15–16, Reap #1*: In Revelation 14:15–16 the angel, a messenger angel, arrives from the temple in heaven for reaping to begin. Christ then begins to reap the earth as the first reaping. No reference to darkness. Angel not identified as having authority over fire, since there is no "clean up" after, it appears those reaped have already been dead.

3) *Revelation 14:17, No work*: In Revelation 14:17 another angel arrives from the temple in heaven and had a sharp sickle, though this angel did not begin using it yet. This will later be shown as the first day of darkness in Joel 2:28–32. There is no reference to a clean-up of blood as in v. 20.

4) *Revelation 14:18–19, Reap #2*: In Revelation 14:18–19 another angel arrives from the temple in heaven. This angel, a second messenger angel, did not have a sickle, though it had authority over fire. He told the previous angel to begin reaping with his sickle. The clusters from the vine of the earth were thrown into the great winepress of the wrath of God. This appears representative as a second reaping. This will later be shown as the second day of darkness in Joel 2:28–32.

5) *Revelation 14:20, Clean-up*: The winepress was trodden outside the city, and blood flowed as high as a horse's bridle for 1,600 stadia. This last event is representative of a clean up after the previous

reaping event #2. Since there is blood remaining, it is expected that those who were killed in vv. 18–19 were previously alive. This author separates this v. 20 clean-up from vv. 18–19 of the bloody battle. No reference to darkness is in v. 20.

Each scriptural event below is numbered as determined by when each angel leaves the temple or altar:

> *Event #1*: Then I looked, and behold, a white cloud, and seated on the cloud one like a son of man, with a golden crown on his head, and a sharp sickle in his hand. (Rev. 14:14)

> *Event #2*: And another angel (first messenger) came out of the temple, calling with a loud voice to him who sat on the cloud, "Put in your sickle, and reap, for the hour to reap has come, for the harvest of the earth is fully ripe." So he who sat on the cloud swung his sickle across the earth, and the earth was reaped. (Rev. 14:15–16)

> *Event #3*: Then another angel came out of the temple in heaven, and he too had a sharp sickle. (Rev. 14:17)

> *Event #4*: And another angel came out from the altar, the angel (second messenger) who has authority over the fire, and he called with a loud voice to the one who had the sharp sickle, "Put in your sickle and gather the clusters from the vine of the earth, for its grapes are ripe." So, the angel swung his sickle across the earth and gathered the grape harvest of the earth and threw it into the great winepress of the wrath of God. (Rev. 14:18–19)

> *Event #5*: And the winepress was trodden outside the city, and blood flowed from the winepress, as high as a horse's bridle, for 1,600 stadia. (Rev. 14:20)

REVELATION 14:14–20 ADDITIONAL OBSERVATIONS

After the first reaping in vv. 15–16 we see there is no "clean up" of blood in v. 17 as with the second reaping of vv. 18–19 with blood in v. 20. Second, the angels in vv. 14–16 are not identified as having control of fire. These two thoughts indicate their actions are against the unrighteous. Joel 2:31–32 (emphasis added) says "The sun shall be turned to darkness, and the moon to blood, *before* the great and awesome day of the LORD (Jehoshaphat battle) comes. And it shall come to pass that everyone who calls on the name of the LORD shall be saved. . . ."

Revelation 14:14–19 indicates the four angels appear to arrive on earth as separate events, though when the battle begins in vv. 18–19, they would all be present as needed in Revelation 9:13–19. Since the two witnesses in Revelation 11:12–13 is described as the last event in the sixth blown trumpet, then these Revelation 14 events seem to occur before. These scriptural five groups are interpreted as occurring on sequentially different days. Supporting this interpretation is that when the two witnesses are dead, they are dead as measured in days, that is for three and a half days in Revelation 11:9, 11. Figures 16, 17 and 18 support the four angels arriving on Day 1,251 (Rev. 14:14), Day 1,252 (Rev. 14:15–16), Day 1,253 (Rev. 14:17), and Day 1,254 (Rev. 9:13–19; 14:18–19). On Day 1,254 is when the fourth and final angel arrives. This last angel is the second messenger, who when he arrives, the battle would begin on that day. Using this daily interpretation, it will be shown these five days chronologically fit before the two witnesses (four-day event) and Israel's rapture (one-day event). All ten days then representing the Days of Awe.

This event of being spiritually saved "before" the day of the Lord (Jehoshaphat battle) is described as a separate and earlier event from the second day of darkness. Since the battle is on Day 1,254 with event #4 in Revelation 14:18–19, then the day before would be Day 1,253. This day is when the Israel remnant would be spiritually saved in Joel 2:31. They would not be raptured until Day 1,260 since there is no rapture type theophany "peals of thunder, rumblings, flashes of lightning" until later in the seventh blown trumpet of Revelation 11:19.

THE REAPERS – LIGHT AND DARKNESS

Revelation 14:14, 16 (first and second separate events) have Christ seated on a white cloud. The white cloud represents light, which is shown later as both Days 1,251 and 1,252. There is no reference to darkness. The two separate events in Revelation 14:17–19 have no reference to a cloud. Comparing to Joel 2:31, there is darkness before the great and awesome day of the Lord. Later in this chapter, the day of the Lord for the Jehoshaphat battle is identified as Day 1,254. Therefore, Days 1,253 and 1,254 would both be darkness.

The sun shall be turned to darkness, and the moon to blood, before the great and awesome day of the LORD comes. And it shall come to pass that everyone who calls on the name of the LORD shall be saved. . . . (Joel 2:31–32)

DAY 1,253 – ISRAEL SPIRITUALLY SAVED

In Joel 2:31–32, great and awesome day of the Lord is the Jehoshaphat battle as previously shown with figure 16. The day before is a representation of anyone, though more specifically Israel, receiving spiritual salvation since the Gentile theophany occurred earlier in Revelation 8:5. If so, then the day Israel is spiritually saved would be in event #3 on Day 1,253 since the day of the Lord (Jehoshaphat battle) is the next day event #4 as Day 1,254.

Beyond Prewrath End–Time Prophecy Chapter 2 discusses that this day of Israel spiritual salvation as the day before the eschatological day of the Lord in the Jehoshaphat battle. Blood, fire, and twenty-four-hour darkness helped place this day of the Lord in the sixth blown trumpet. Many scholars place this day of the Lord in the sixth opened seal with its Wrath of the Lamb, though there is no blood (death) or fire there.

DAY 1,254 – ALL FOUR ANGELS ARRIVE IN TIME FOR BATTLE

The third row of figure 18 represents all four angels arriving on different days. First angel of Revelation 14:14 arrives on Day 1,251; second angel of Revelation 14:15 arrives on Day 1,252; third angel of Revelation 14:17 arrives on Day 1,253; and the last angel of Revelation 14:18 arrives on the day of battle as Day 1,254. On this last day all angels would have arrived on earth for the Jehoshaphat battle. Revelation 9:15, which says, "So the four angels, who had been prepared for the hour, the day, the month, and the year, were released to kill a third of mankind," is representative of fallen angels.

Therefore, the hypothesis of each event lasting one day provides a good fit from this limited verification analysis.

DAY 1,254 – JEHOSHAPHAT BATTLE – FIGURE 18

The day of the Lord in Joel 3:2 is identified as the Jehoshaphat battle since the battle occurs in the valley of Jehoshaphat. This is the second of Jesus's eschatological battles. All three of Jesus's battles could be called a campaign

Ten Days of Awe 67

for his second coming. Figure 18 shows rows two to nine with commonalities among the Scriptures. This helps to link them to the Jehoshaphat battle reaping of Revelation 14:18–19 as part of the sixth blown trumpet:

1) Location of the battle is Jehoshaphat,
2) Sixth blown trumpet,
3) Occurs in sixth blown trumpet,
4) Two pairs of four angels, one fallen and one not, are present by the Jehoshaphat battle on Day 1,254,
5) Winepress overflows with wickedness,
6) Darkness,
7) Day of the Lord,
8) Fire,
9) Day of Lord – Wrath of God, and
10) Horsemen.

These common thoughts tie Joel 3:1–2, 9–16, and Revelation 9:13–19 with event #4 of Revelation 14:18–19 as the Jehoshaphat battle. Scholars place the Jehoshaphat Valley in the Kidron Valley on the east side of Jerusalem.[1] This could indicate that the Antichrist's army attack from the east where in Zechariah 14:4 the Mount of Olives was previously formed on Day 1 into a "very wide valley." Another supporting reason is Zechariah 14:8 where Jerusalem has living water flowing either west or east out of Jerusalem. Previous blown trumpets have much of the world's water supply polluted.

> On that day his feet shall stand on the Mount of Olives that lies before Jerusalem on the east, and the Mount of Olives shall be split in two from east to west by a *very wide valley*, so that one half of the Mount shall move northward, and the other half southward. (Zech. 14:4, emphasis added)

---

1 Robert Van Kampen, *The Sign of Christ's Coming and the End of the Age*, Published by Crossway Books, a publishing ministry of Good News Publishers, 1300 Crescent Street, Wheaton, Illinois 60187, 1992, 289–290.

On that day *living waters* shall flow out from Jerusalem, half of them to the eastern sea and half of them to the western sea. It shall continue in summer as in winter. (Zech. 14:8, emphasis added)

FIGURE 18: JEHOSHAPHAT BATTLE

Isaiah and Joel	Revelation 9	Revelation 11; 14:14–20	Malachi 4
The Valley of Jehoshaphat (Joel 3:2)			
Trumpet blown; Bridegroom leaves his room (Joel 2:15–16)	Blown trumpet 6 (v. 13)	Prior to start of blown trumpet 7 (11:15)	
	Four angels (v. 14)	Four angels (14:14–15, 17–18)	
Sickle; winepress overflowing because evil is great (Joel 3:13)		Sharp sickle; winepress of the wrath of God (14:17, 19)	
Sun darkened before the day of the Lord (Joel 2:31)		No reference to clouds (darkness) (14:17–19)	
Day of the Lord (Joel 3:14)		Wrath of God (14:19)	"The day is coming" (v. 1)
Blood and fire; year of recompense and soil into sulfur (Isa. 34:8–9; Joel 2:30)	Fire, smoke, and sulfur (vv. 17–18)	Authority of third angel over fire (14:18)	Evildoers set ablaze (v. 1)
	One-third of mankind killed (v. 18)	Blood up to a horse's bridle (14:20)	Wicked tread down (v. 3)
	Horsemen (vv. 16–17)	Horse bridle (indicates horsemen) (14:20)	

DAY 1,254 – JEHOSHAPHAT BATTLE WITH RIDERS ON HORSES

The sixth blown trumpet battle is identified in Revelation 9:13. In Revelation 9:7 and Joel 2:4, the riders have horses with breastplates that were fiery red. Joel 3:2 identifies this battle as the Jehoshaphat battle. In Revelation 9:13–19 and Revelation 14:18, the angels caused the Lord's wrath. The wrath is severe enough that one-third of mankind dies in Revelation 9:15. The angel with the sickle, who arrived earlier in event #3 of Revelation 14:17, appears to reap the wicked who died during this battle event #4 of Revelation 14:18–19. This is since there is blood being cleaned up in Revelation 14:20 (post reap #2), though not in Revelation 14:17 (post reap #1). This looks like a team effort between the Jehoshaphat battle with the four angels on Day 1,254 and the next day clean up with the riders on the horses. Revelation 9:13–19 is a much more detailed description of event #4 (Jehoshaphat battle) than in Revelation 14:18–19.

The battle appears to occur before the two witnesses are killed on earth. Revelation 11:10 has the wicked celebrating by exchanging presents. It is unlikely for the wicked to have a celebration when two hundred million mounted riders caused the Lord's wrath in Revelation 9:16–17. The witness's five-day (Passover to Day 1) timeline of chapter 7 figure 11 supports them being killed at the start of Day 1,256 then being dead for three and a half days before being called up here to heaven as described in Revelation 11:3–13.

DAY 1,255 – DAY AFTER JEHOSHAPHAT BATTLE

After the Jehoshaphat battle is when the blood flowed outside the city with the use of horses in Revelation 14:20. During this time the Jews tread down the wicked under the soles of their feet in Malachi 4:2–3. Those who are trampled down are those likely with the mark of the beast and who worshiped the beast and its image.

> But for you who fear my name, the sun of righteousness shall rise with healing in its wings. You shall go out leaping like calves from the stall. And you shall tread down the wicked, for they will be ashes under the soles of your feet, on the day when I act, says the LORD of hosts. (Mal. 4:2–3)

ISRAEL RAPTURED AT THE END OF SEVENTIETH WEEK

Figure 18 previously harmonized the Jehoshaphat battle as part of the sixth blown trumpet using many Scriptures. This could not be done with the poured bowls. The second great eschatological theophany of Revelation 11:19, in the seventh blown trumpet, supports this Scripture as a rapture event. Since we know Israel is provided (and protected) for 1,260 days starting on Day 1, this supports the seventh blown trumpet as occurring on Day 1,260. The third eschatological great theophany of Revelation 16:18 in the seventh poured bowl would seemingly end on Day 1,290 (Dan. 12:11–12). This third rapture event is representative of the sheep and goats (Matt. 25:31–46).

A second supporting reason that Israel is raptured in Revelation 11:19 is that the two witnesses are taken to heaven in the earlier sixth blown trumpet. Why are they taken? It appears their mission to prophesy in Revelation 11:3 for the 1,260 days has been completed.

DAYS 1,256 TO 1,259 – PART OF THE SIXTH TRUMPET, TWO WITNESSES

The two witnesses will prophesy for 1,260 days in Revelation 11:3. After they finish their testimony, they are killed by the beast in v. 7. Then in v. 9 those on earth will "look" at their dead bodies for three and a half days since they were not permitted to bury them. Since they were looking at their bodies for three and a half days, it appears there was daylight. Those who dwell on the earth will rejoice, make merry, and exchange presents in vv. 7–10. After they come back to life they were taken to heaven and there was an earthquake in vv. 11–13. The Bible said they were dead for three and a half days, though it did not say how long after coming back to life before being called to heaven. It did not reference this duration, though referencing the three and a half days points to the duration of vv. 11–13 as being much less. Therefore, this duration is assigned as a day or less. Chapter 7 provides additional support to this assumption with the two witnesses likely to arrive on the Passover, five days before the abomination on Day 1. Figure 11 in Chapter 7 shows this great five-day chronological fit.

This means after the two witnesses finish their testimony and are killed, they were likely on earth a total of 1,264 days. 1,260 days witnessing, three and a half days dead, and half a day alive before being called up to heaven. These last four days of the sixth blown trumpet appear to match Days 1,256 to 1,259, which will be shown to exactly fit within the ten Days of Awe of Days 1,251 to 1,260.

DAY 1,260 – SEVENTH TRUMPET, ISRAEL PHYSICALLY SAVED

We see the same great eschatology theophany with its *lightning flashes* in Revelation 11:19 for the seventh blown trumpet as for the one-day rapture of the elect in Revelation 8:5 in the seventh opened seal. Both Scriptures are the last verse of each septet. Since the exact same one-day rapture language in Revelation 8:5 is used, therefore, it is probable that Revelation 11:19 will also be a one-day event.

It appears before Israel's last day of protection from the dragon Satan is over in Revelation 12:14 that Israel would be raptured on Day 1,260 to Jerusalem and not to heaven. This location is deduced since the second rejoicing in heaven is not until Revelation 19:1–4. This is eight chapters after Israel's rapture in Revelation 11:19, which points to the rapture location being earthly. Luke 17:24 lightning flashes are representative of the return of the Son of Man, which is also in Revelation 11:19. These lightning flashes (with the same theophany though without the earthquake) are emanating from the throne in Revelation 4:5 with the Lord in vv. 9–11 identified as seated on the throne. Therefore, are representative of what the rabbinic (Jewish scholars) manuscripts describe as the Shekinah glory.

> For as the *lightning flashes* (means of rapture from the earth to meet Jesus in the sky) and lights up the sky from one side to the other, *so will the Son of Man* (Jesus) *be in his day.* (Luke 17:24, emphasis added)

> But the woman was given the two wings of the great eagle so that she might fly from the serpent into the wilderness, to the place where she is to be nourished for a time, and times, and half a time. (Rev. 12:14)

> Then God's temple in heaven was opened, and the ark of his covenant was seen within his temple. There were *flashes of lightning*, rumblings, peals of thunder, an earthquake, and heavy hail. (Rev. 11:19, emphasis added)

WEDDING AND MARRIAGE SUPPER OF THE LAMB

In the Jehoshaphat battle in Joel 2:15–16, the sixth blown trumpet said the wedding ceremony was about to begin. Using the feasts of the Lord theory, this was identified as Day 1,254. Of course, the wedding ceremony must be held prior to the marriage supper. This fits in well with the wedding occurring in Revelation 19:7 and the marriage supper of the Lamb immediately after in Revelation 19:9.

The earlier reference in Revelation 19:6 is where John heard what sounded like a great multitude (bride), like the roar of rushing waters and like loud peals of thunder (groom), shouting. This appears in the same reference as Revelation 16:18, which is in the seventh blown trumpet. Earlier chapters have identified this as Day 1,260. Joel 2:15–16 saying the wedding ceremony was about to begin on Day 1,254, then it occurring six days later, provides a reasonable fit.

God's voice is described in Scripture as the sound or roar of rushing waters:

> And behold, the glory of the God of Israel was coming from the east. And the sound of his coming was like the *sound of many waters*, and the earth shone with his glory. (Ezek. 43:2, emphasis added)

> For as the *lightning* comes from the east and shines as far as the west, so will be the coming of the Son of Man. (Matt. 24:27, emphasis added)

> [H]is feet were like burnished bronze, refined in a furnace, and *his voice was like the roar of many waters*. (Rev. 1:15, emphasis added)

ONE YEAR HONEYMOON

"When a man is newly married, he shall not go out with the army or be liable for any other public duty. He shall be free at home one year to be happy with his wife whom he has taken." (Deut. 24:5). The Lord (groom) must have at least one year with the bride before returning to go to war. This is great for the elect raptured in Revelation 8:5 to heaven where they are rejoicing in Revelation 7.

What about the Jewish nation, which will be raptured and the wedding on Day 1,260? They are also part of the one bride of Christ with the Gentiles and would need to have a year with the groom. The Armageddon battle with Jesus and the armies of heaven would be in battle only a few weeks later in the sixth poured bowl. One possible solution to this required one-year honeymoon may be that they are spending time in heaven and not on earth with its slower duration. After the earthly béma in Jerusalem, it seems the bride and groom must go to heaven for necessary time dilation to obtain the one year. Chapter 3 of *Beyond Prewrath End–Time Prophecy* provides supporting details of this time dilation.

The marriage begins at the béma in Revelation 11:18 in the seventh blown trumpet. Therefore, with the heaven time dilation, the groom (the Lord) would have at least one year with the bride (the Church and Israel) before returning for war in Armageddon.

CONCLUSION

This analysis indicates that the ten days leading up to Israel's physical rapture may be the Days of Awe for the sixth and seventh blown trumpets. The first five days are from 1,251 to 1,255. Days 1,252 and 1,254 are the harvest in the sixth blown trumpet. The Jews being spiritually saved on Day 1,253.

The next four days from 1,256 to 1,259 being the death and rapture of the two witnesses also in the sixth blown trumpet. The last Day 1,260 is when Israel is physically raptured in the seventh blown trumpet.

These ten days provide a perfect fit to the ten Days of Awe as shown in figure 16!

1) Days 1,251 – 1,255: Five days of Revelation 14:14–20.
2) Days 1,256 – 1,259: Four days of Revelation 11:7–12.
3) Day 1,260: One–day of Revelation 11:19.

Chapter 12

Conclusion

Figure 19 shows that the beginning of the seventieth week of Daniel may occur on one of the following 24-hour Jewish days: 13 November 2023 or 9 November 2026. These two dates have been narrowed from the list of annual dates using all the filters. The figure is written such that if the reader disagrees with any filter, then they could easily discount that column to reflect their own unique perspective. If the reader discounts all filters except counting back 2,519 days from the respective future Yom Kippur date, then all the first column annual dates would be viable. All dates range from about mid-October to mid-November.

Another possibility is 23 to 24 October 2063.[1] This is based on when the temple was destroyed in 70 AD and this second generation, starting when the Israel military took control of the temple mount on 7 June 1967. This can only be possible if the Israel lifespan is able to reach at least 103 years by 2070. For this to occur, something extraordinary like a cure for cancer would be needed. Note, the 75-day filter was not met.

We should all be observant of a multi-national agreement being signed with Israel on one of the specific annual dates identified in the first column of figures 19 and 20. It is assumed that the final treaty ratification date would occur when Israel and at least one other party's signature occur on one of these dates. In Daniel 9:26–27 we see the prince "shall make a strong covenant." Some adamantly say this means he will sign or initiate the covenant. Scripture does not specifically say this, though it is certainly possible. One way to add strength could be to provide a UN type enforcement during the seven-year treaty (2,520 days) or financial support.

Since all prophecy is Israel centric, these dates should be measured with Jerusalem time zone. Consider that Jerusalem and Israel are described as the "center of the earth" in Ezekiel 38:12. This is likely a reflection of Zechariah 14:8 and Revelation 22:1–2 with two rivers emanating from the throne in Jerusalem, one to the east and one to the west. Each Jewish day

---

1 Hebcal.com, "Jewish Holidays 2070", accessed March 28, 2021, https://www.hebcal.com/holidays/2070.

begins shortly after sunset in Jerusalem after the first three stars are seen. Sunset in Jerusalem for October to November is about 4:40 p.m. to 4:43 p.m.

> [T]o seize spoil and carry off plunder, to turn your hand against the waste places that are now inhabited, and the people who were gathered from the nations, who have acquired livestock and goods, *who dwell at the center of the earth.* (Ezek. 38:12, emphasis added)

> On that day living waters shall flow out from Jerusalem, half of them to the eastern sea and half of them to the western sea. It shall continue in summer as in winter. (Zech. 14:8)

Figures 19 and 20 referenced data sources can be found in:

1) First column, beginning of seventieth week dates: See figure 6 in chapter 4.
2) Second column, Day 1: See figure 10 in chapter 7.
3) Third column, Filter #1 for two thousand years: See figure 9 in chapter 6.
4) Fourth column, Filter #2 for two witnesses arriving on the Passover, five days before Day 1: See figure 10 in chapter 7.
5) Fifth column, Filter #3 for 75 days from Day 1,261 to 1,335: See figure 13 in chapter 8.
6) Sixth column, Filter for Israel's second–generation lifespan age: See chapter 9.

Conclusion

FIGURE 19: OVERVIEW – BASED ON 14 MAY 1948 BIRTH

Start of 70th week	Day 1	Filter #1 2000 Year	Filter #2 5 Days	Filter #3 75 Days	Age Day 1,260
10/28/19	4/10/23	No	Yes	Yes	78.4
11/16/20	4/29/24	Yes	No	Yes	79.4
11/6/21	4/19/25	No	No	No	80.4
10/26/22	4/8/26	No	No	No	81.3
11/13/23	*4/26/27*	*Yes*	Yes	Yes	82.4
11/2/24	4/15/28	No	Yes	No	83.4
10/22/25	4/4/29	No	Yes	No	84.3
11/09/26	*4/22/30*	*Yes*	Yes	Yes	85.4
10/30/27	4/12/31	No	Yes	Yes	Too old
11/18/28	5/1/32	No	No	No	Too old
11/7/29	4/20/33	Yes	No	No	Too old

FIGURE 20: OVERVIEW – BASED ON 7 JUNE 1967 BIRTH

Start of 70th week	Day 1	Filter #1 2000 Year	Filter #2 5 Days	Filter #3 75 Days	Age Day 1,260
10/23/63	4/5/67	Yes	Yes	No	103.2

JEWISH CALENDAR

As discussed in chapter 3, Mitchell First book has the Rabbinic (Jewish) vs conventional (Gregorian) chronology short by 207 years. If so, this points to the 70th week start as occurring during their corrected year 5993 (2786 + 207, seven years short of 6000) from 1 October 2025 to 30 September 2026.

FIGURE 21: BEGINNING OF SEVENTIETH WEEK OF DANIEL

Start of 70th week (24-hour window)	Gregorian Date on Day 1,260	Jewish Year on Day 1,260
26 to 27 Oct. 2022	18 Sep. 2029	5790
13 to 14 Nov. 2023	6 Oct. 2030	5791
2 to 3 Nov. 2024	26 Sep. 2031	5792
22 to 23 Oct. 2025	14 Sep. 2032	5793
9 to 10 Nov. 2026	2 Oct. 2033	5794
30 to 31 Oct. 2027	22 Sep. 2034	5795
18 to 19 Nov. 2028	12 Oct. 2035	5796
23 to 24 Oct. 2063	15 Sep. 2070	5831

JEWISH SABBATH YEAR

The Jewish year ends on Day 1,250 the day before the Feast of Trumpets. This day would be the last day in the Jewish month of Elul. Tishri 1 would begin the next day on Day 1,251. Kevin Howard and Marvin Rosenthal's book *The Feasts of the Lord* directly associated the rapture with the Feast of Trumpets. A second day of watchfulness by the rabbis is reflective of the two-day window for the rapture. This two-day "window" is what *Beyond Prewrath End-Time Prophecy* chapter 3 is based on.

> It occurs at the New Moon when only the slightest crescent is visible. However, clouds could obscure the moon, and witnesses were required in ancient days. Watchfulness was a critical ingredient of this feast. The rabbis later added a second day to this feast to make sure they did not miss it. This need for watchfulness and preparedness in connection with the Feast of Trumpets is echoed and reechoed throughout the New Testament in connection with Messiah's coming.[2]

---

2   Kevin Howard and Marvin Rosenthal, *The Feasts of the Lord: God's Prophetic Calendar from Calvary to the Kingdom* (Nashville: Thomas Nelson, 1997), 28.

SIXTH MILLENNIUM ENDS

Israel is raptured in Revelation 11:19 on Day 1,260 with the second great eschatological theophany. This rapture is prophesized with Hosea 6:1–2 when on the third day Israel will live in the Lord's presence. 2 Peter 3:8 represents these two days with the Lord as two thousand years. Their earthly rapture is representative of being in the Lord's presence.

> Come, let us return to the Lord;
> for he has torn us, that he may heal us;
> he has struck us down, and he will bind us up.
> After two days he will revive us;
> on the third day he will raise us up,
> that we may live before him. (Hos. 6:1–2)

> But do not overlook this one fact, beloved, that with the Lord one day is as a thousand years, and a thousand years as one day. (2 Pet. 3:8)

WHEN DOES THE SEVENTH MILLENNIUM START?

Day 1,335 is considered the start of the seventh millennium with Jesus starting to reign on earth for one thousand years in Revelation 20:4. Robert Van Kampen in *The Sign of Christ's Coming and the End of the Age* supports this.[3] These 1,335 days are supported with Daniel 12:12.

CHRISTMAS AND HANUKKAH

It is recognized that Christmas and Hanukkah days are celebrated each year. They only overlap one time over the next 28 years. This overlap is in 2027 with an eighteen-hour celebration overlap. If the beginning of the seventieth week of Daniel starts in 2023, then the first year of the great tribulation, Christians and Jews would be celebrating both events on 25 December 2027! Hanukkah starts on 24 December 2027 shortly after sunset until about 24 hours later. Both celebrations overlap from 12:01 a.m. on 25 December until shortly after sunset on 25 December.

---

3 Robert Van Kampen, *The Sign of Christ's Coming and the End of the Age*, Published by Crossway Books, a publishing ministry of Good News Publishers, 1300 Crescent Street, Wheaton, Illinois 60187, 1992, 474.

DATES WHEN THE GREAT TRIBULATION ENDS

We know the window duration of the sixth and seventh opened seals based on *Beyond Prewrath End-Time Prophecy* chapters 3 and 4, and when each annual Feast of Trumpets occurs. Therefore, we can determine a window each year when the sixth seal could begin. The opening of the sixth seal would be confirmed when normal night and day of the fifth seal turns into the 24-hour darkness of the sixth opened seal (Matt. 24:29; Rev. 6:12).

In figure 22 we see the parallels with Revelation 6, 8, and Matthew 24 for the seven opened seals and the first blown trumpet. *Beyond Prewrath End–Time Prophecy* chapter 4 proposes the sixth opened seal duration was from 27 to 32 days. This is a six-day window. *Beyond Prewrath End–Time Prophecy* chapter 3 proposes the rapture to occur at the end of the seventh opened seal in Revelation 8:5 on either the seventh or eighth day. This is a two-day window. Combining both opened seal window durations, there becomes a seven-day window range from the highest range of 34 (27 + 7) to the lowest range of 40 (32 + 8) as to when the great tribulation could end. That is, once we enter the 24-hour darkness, the rapture of the elect would occur as early as 34 days or as late as 40 days.

Figure 24 shows this seven-day window for various years in either July or August. For example, say the start of the seventieth week is 13 November 2023. Then there would be three possible years with a seven-day window whether the great tribulation has ended and the sixth opened seal has begun with its 24-hour darkness. The three window dates would be 22 to 28 August 2027 (first window year), 11 to 17 August 2028 (second window year), or 31 July to 6 August 2029 (third window year).

> When he opened the sixth seal, I looked, and behold, there was a great earthquake, and the sun became black as sackcloth, the full moon became like blood, (Rev. 6:12)

FIGURE 22: PARALLELS BETWEEN MATTHEW 24 AND REVELATION 6–8

Matthew 24	Parallels	Revelation 6, 8
vv. 4–5	Peaceful conquest (birth pangs)	Opened seal 1 (6:1–2)
vv. 6–7	Wars (birth pangs)	Opened seal 2 (6:3–4)
v. 7	Famines and earthquakes (birth pangs)	Opened seal 3 (6:5–6)
vv. 9–14	Death and tribulation (hard labor)	Opened seal 4 (6:7–8)
vv. 15–26	Martyrdom and great tribulation (hard labor)	Opened seal 5 (6:9–11)
v. 29	Wrath of the Lamb (no tribulation)	Opened seal 6 (6:12–17)
vv. 30–31, 37–42	Normal life, then rapture (no tribulation)	Opened seal 7 ("ready") (8:1–5)
vv. 37–42	Trumpets prepared and first trumpet blown till poured bowls are emptied (wrath of God)	Blown trumpet 1 ("aim" and "fire") (8:6ff.)

FIGURE 23: BEYOND PREWRATH OVERVIEW TIMELINE

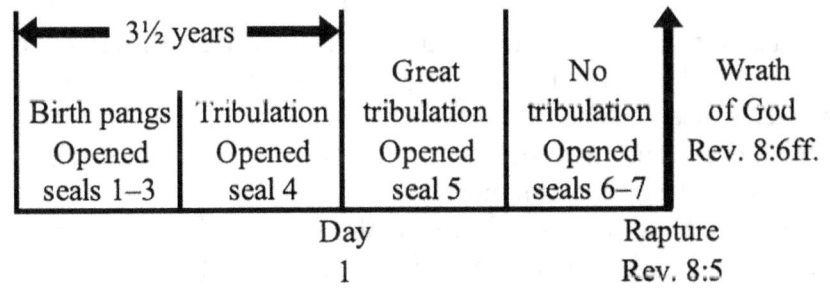

FIGURE 24: WINDOW DATES WHEN GREAT TRIBULATION ENDS CONFIRMED WITH 24 HOUR DARKNESS

Window Opens	Window Closes	Tishri 1
13 Aug. 2025	19 Aug. 2025	22 Sep. 2025
2 Aug. 2026	8 Aug. 2026	11 Sep. 2026
22 Aug. 2027	28 Aug. 2027	1 Oct. 2027
11 Aug. 2028	17 Aug. 2028	20 Sep. 2028
31 Jul. 2029	6 Aug. 2029	9 Sep. 2029
18 Aug. 2030	24 Aug. 2030	27 Sep 2030
8 Aug. 2031	14 Aug. 2031	17 Sep. 2031
27 Jul. 2032	2 Aug. 2032	5 Sep. 2032
6 Aug. 2069	12 Aug. 2069	15 Sep. 2069
27 Jul. 2070	2 Aug. 2070	5 Sep. 2070
14 Aug. 2071	20 Aug. 2071	23 Sep. 2071

FURY DURATION = A LITTLE WHILE

It is proposed the *little while* of Isaiah 26:20 is chronologically parallel to Revelation 6:11 *little while*. A *little while* is referenced 29 times in the ESV. At least five times are in reference to a short amount of time measured in hours (1 Kings 18:45; Matt. 26:73; Mark 14:70; Acts 5:34; Heb. 10:37). One was with Satan (Rev. 20:3). About nine were too difficult to determine where in prophecy they are located or even to approximate their duration.

The Scriptures (John 12:35; 13:33; 14:19; 16:16–18; Heb. 2:7, 2:9) appear to have a common theme relative to the apostles not seeing Jesus again for a "little while," which was measured in days. This little while duration appear to have relevance to determine the duration of the fury just before the great tribulation ends. This analysis assumes the little while fury of Isaiah 26:20 is measured in days and not in hours.

Jesus used the words *a little while* in John 14:19 and 16:16–19 in reference to the time from His crucifixion until His ascension (Acts 1:3). The John MacArthur ESV Study Bible on John 16:16–18 confirms this understanding. This duration is, therefore, 40 days.

Conclusion

The first reference is plainly to the brief period between the crucifixion and the resurrection of Jesus, and the second reference is to the resurrection appearances (the "little while" after which the disciples will see Jesus again). The phrase is repeated by both Jesus and the disciples (vv. 17–19), recalling four previous instances of "a little while" in John's Gospel (cf. 7:33; 12:35; 13:33; 14:19)[4]

> He presented himself alive to them after his suffering by many proofs, appearing to them during *forty days* and speaking about the kingdom of God. (Acts 1:3, emphasis added)

Satan is captured in Revelation 20:1–3 and put on a chain for a thousand years. After this he is released for a little while before the millennium ends.

Chapter 11 of *Beyond Prewrath End–Time Prophecy* proposed that Satan was captured on Day 1,289 or 1,290.[5] This assumption was supported since Satan would be expected to otherwise cause another battle on earth.

This author considers that when the third and last great eschatological theophany rapture occurs in Revelation 16:18 on Day 1,290 that the only humans still living on earth are those who worship the beast and its image and have the mark of the beast. Since Satan has conquered all those remaining on earth, there is no need for him to be at war before being chained. Though, Revelation 19:20 (with the beast being captured) and 20:1–3 point to the duration of this "little while" as possibly 46 days.

We now recognize that this *little while* duration is 40 to 46 days.

> Yet a *little while* and the world will see me no more, but you will see me. Because I live, you also will live. (John 14:19, emphasis added)

> A *little while*, and you will see me no longer; and again a little while, and you will see me. (John 16:16, emphasis added)

The NASB translation of Revelation 6:11 has *a little while*. Consider this fifth opened seal v. 11 is the last verse of the great tribulation in vv. 9–11.

---

4 John MacArthur ESV Study Bible, Crossway, Wheaton, Illinois, © 2008, 2234.

5 Robert Parker, *Beyond Prewrath End–Time Prophecy*, Robert's Trumpet LLC, © 2022, 149.

The context helps to fit Isaiah 26:20 hiding until the increased persecution ends.

> And a white robe was given to each of them; and they were told that they were to rest for a *little while* longer, until the number of their fellow servants and their brothers and sisters who were to be killed even as they had been, was completed also. (Rev. 6:11 NASB, emphasis added)

PERSECUTION GETS WORSE JUST BEFORE IT ENDS

In Isaiah 26:20, the fury is so bad that the Lord requests his people to hide in their chambers, likely with their doors locked, for a little while until it has passed. A chamber is synonymous with a present-day room. As we know, a house has many rooms. When the fury ends, the great tribulation seems to be over. Therefore, just before the great tribulation ends, the persecution will be worse for 40 to 46 days.

> Come, my people, enter your chambers, and shut your doors behind you; hide yourselves for a *little while* until the fury has passed by. (Isa. 26:20, emphasis added)

The rapture may not occur in the first "rapture window" year of the great tribulation as shown in figure 7. So, it is possible that believers may need to hide for two or possibly three times. That is, we could be hiding in the first and possibly the second year when the fury does not happen. Each hiding duration being a maximum of 52 (46+ (7−1)) days. This allows for the 46-day maximum fury and the seven-day window of the sixth and seventh opened seals. To go outside to verify for certain whether we are in the fury would be too dangerous.

I suspect that we will recognize the fury has begun when those with the mark of the beast and who worship the beast and its image are persistent at knocking at our residences. To some degree this persistent knocking is a blessing since it means we are within about 80 days of meeting Jesus in the sky. No one should open an outside door, become visible to them from the inside, or respond verbally to them. When they appear, it is probably best to move quietly to the furthest location in the house from the outside door(s). If the dog barks, then fine. As far as they know, the owner of the house could have the mark of the beast, and worship the beast and its image. So, if they did try to forcibly enter, they could be met with the homeowner's legitimate deadly force. Those being persecuted during this fury will likely have few, if any, constitutional rights.

THE FURY ENDS WHEN?

There are two reasons we will know when the danger of a fury has passed. First, when the sixth opened seal begins there is 24-hour darkness.

The second reason that the fury has passed is when figure 25 second column date has passed. Not having the 24-hour darkness would indicate that the fury never started and the great tribulation would continue until about ten and half months later when another fury window opens. This figure builds on the previous figure 24.

FIGURE 25: WHEN TO BEGIN AND END HIDING IN YOUR CHAMBER

Fury Starts (Earliest Date)	Fury Ends (Latest Date) or as confirmed by 24 hour darkness
28 Jun. 2025	19 Aug. 2025
17 Jun. 2026	8 Aug. 2026
7 Jul. 2027	28 Aug. 2027
26 Jun. 2028	17 Aug. 2028
15 Jun. 2029	6 Aug. 2029
3 Jul. 2030	24 Aug. 2030
23 Jun. 2031	14 Aug. 2031
11 Jun. 2032	2 Aug. 2032
21 Jun. 2069	12 Aug. 2069
11 Jun. 2070	2 Aug. 2070
29 Jun. 2071	20 Aug. 2071

As discussed before, this is a maximum window hiding duration of 52 (46 + (7–1)) days to hide from the fury.

FIGURE 26: FIFTH SEAL TO FIRST TRUMPET

Great tribulation		No tribulation		
Light		Darkness	Light	
← Seal 5 →		Seal 6	Seal 7	Trumpet 1
	Fury			Wrath
	(Hide)			of God
Day 1	40 to 46 days	27 to 32 days	7 or 8 days	Rev. 8:7
		Great Earthquake and Darkness Rev. 6:12 Matt. 24:29	Rapture Rev. 8:5 then Rev. 7	

PERSECUTION ENDS WITH LAST TWO SEALS THEN STARTS AGAIN

The tribulation ending with the sixth opened seal and continuing into the seventh opened seal is an opportunity for both Jews and Christians to escape from their location of persecution. Unfortunately, since the Jews will not be raptured until the end of the seventh blown trumpet, it means they will have 34 to 40 days to relocate to a safe location before the first trumpet of Revelation 8:7 is blown. This is since idols are known to exist later during the sixth blown trumpet of Revelation 9:20–21 and will likely appear again much sooner during the blown trumpets.

> Immediately after the *tribulation* of those days the sun will be darkened, and the moon will not give its light, and the stars will fall from heaven, and the powers of the heavens will be shaken. (Matt. 24:29, emphasis added)

The rest of mankind, who were not killed by these plagues, did not repent of the works of their hands nor give up worshiping demons and idols of gold and silver and bronze and stone and wood, which cannot see or hear or walk, nor did they repent of their murders or their sorceries or their sexual immorality or their thefts. (Rev. 9:20–21)

PROPERTY TAXES

Persecution is likely to extend to paying property taxes. Taxes should be paid as soon as possible every year for the following two reasons. First, is it is expected that the great tribulation tempo will increase as time elapses, especially when entering the fury.

Second, the earlier you pay your taxes the greater the chance property owners can pay with something other than the mark of the beast. This exception is likely to be abolished some time into the great tribulation. When receiving your tax notice, examine it closely to determine whether payment can be made with something other than the mark. Payment made without entering into the building is strongly desired.

American Eagle gold and silver coins may be accepted as payment. Having a few 90 percent silver U.S. minted coins could be used for smaller change. I recommend avoiding the Roosevelt dimes and having the older Barber dimes since they are easily recognizable as 90 percent silver content.

Consider without having a structure to live in for 46 days it would not be possible to hide in your chamber-room to Scripturally avoid the fury (Isa. 26:20). The third angel warning (Rev. 14:9–11) on Day 1 should be enough to cause people to think twice before taking the mark of beast to buy or sell, at least until one's household's pantry is empty. Hunger may eventually cause some to relent and take the mark of the beast for currency needed to buy and sell though there are eternal hades consequences if they also worship the beast and its image.

COMFORT FOR BELIEVERS

If you are overwhelmed after reading this book, I would like to provide words of comfort.

> Here is a call for the *endurance* of the saints, those who keep the commandments of God and their faith in Jesus. (Rev. 14:12, emphasis added)

First, not all nations will be under the Antichrist control since wars will continue to the end (Dan. 9:26). If there are wars on the earth, then he has not conquered all of the earth (Rev. 6:8). His authority is a quarter of the earth. For believers, the way to mitigate persecution would be to avoid living under his geographical area of authority. This geographic location would be expected to be those countries around Israel. Several of these countries seem to be described in Ezekiel 30:5–6.

> Cush, and Put, and Lud, and all Arabia, and Libya, and the people of the land that is in league, shall fall with them by the sword. "Thus says the Lord: Those who support Egypt shall fall. . . ." (Ezek. 30:5–6)

> And after the sixty-two weeks, an anointed one shall be cut off and shall have nothing. And the people of the prince who is to come shall destroy the city and the sanctuary. Its end shall come with a flood, and *to the end there shall be war.* Desolations are decreed. (Dan. 9:26, emphasis added)

> And I looked, and behold, a pale horse! And its rider's name was Death, and Hades followed him. And they were given *authority over a fourth of the earth*, to kill with sword and with famine and with pestilence and by wild beasts of the earth. (Rev. 6:8, emphasis added)

Second, Daniel 11:39 has the strongest of fortresses being dealt with. This could include being attacked, though being dealt with should be thought of in a more general sense. It could include restricting commercial goods, such as oil, grains, and wine.

> *He shall deal with the strongest fortresses* with the help of a foreign god. Those who acknowledge him he shall load with honor. He shall make them rulers over many and shall divide the land for a price (Dan. 11:39, emphasis added)

Third, the great tribulation will be cut short, which will shorten its duration. (Matt. 24:22).

Conclusion

Fourth, ability to know when to hide from the fury near the end of the great tribulation should provide great comfort.

Fifth, endurance of saints is needed. Consider anyone who refuses to take the mark of the beast will be unable to buy or sell (Rev. 13:16–17). By definition this means those will need to become preppers, whether ready or not. Preparation is the key to providing nourishment and medication for your body to survive. The overall theme for believers living through the tribulation is endurance (Matt. 24:13; Rev. 14:12) with the coming blessed hope (Titus 2:13).

Sixth, we see a woman who is seated on a beast in Revelation 17:3. Verse 5 identifies her as Babylon-the mother of prostitutes with abominations. There is a mutual bond between the woman and the beast. The bond is broken when the beast and ten horns turn on the woman (Rev. 17:16). Attacking one of their own will distract the ten king's military force for a short period of time. This is expected to slow down, though not stop Israel's off-spring (the Church) from being persecuted as prophesized in Revelation 12:17.

Jesus's Jerusalem battle on Day 1 should be considered a counter attack against Gog and the ten-king coalition since they attacked first. Jesus's counter attack will only be focused on the force attacking Israel. It will not be against the force attacking Babylon, since God put it into their hearts. Jesus attacking only part of the force should be expected to slow down the great tribulation advancement, though not stop it.

> And the ten horns that you saw, they and the beast will hate the prostitute. They will make her desolate and naked, and devour her flesh and burn her up with fire, for God has put it into their hearts to carry out his purpose by being of one mind and handing over their royal power to the beast, until the words of God are fulfilled. (Rev. 17:16–17)

Seventh, if you get the mark there is nothing in Scripture (that I know of) which says it is not possible to remove it. Unless, you probably worship the beast, its image and receive their mark. Though I would not recommend someone test this understanding. On Day 1 it would become evident to all when the world-wide third angel warning in Revelation 14:9–11 is given of the consequences of taking the mark and worshiping the beast and its image (cf. 2 Thess. 2:9–12). The desire to remove it would then become obvious to all, especially Christians. The removal may require a physician, possibly a Christian.

BLASPHEMY OF THE HOLY SPIRIT

Jesus says in Matthew 12:32 NASB "And whoever speaks a word against the Son of Man, it shall be forgiven him; but whoever speaks against the Holy Spirit, it shall not be forgiven him, either in this age or in the age to come." What words of blasphemy against the Holy Spirit was Jesus talking about?

Consider 1 Timothy 4:1–2 NASB that in "later times" they are "devoting themselves to deceitful spirits". This seems to be the same thought as the third angel saying "If anyone *worships the beast and his image*, and receives a mark on his forehead or on his hand." (Rev. 14:9 NASB, emphasis added). As a consequence, v. 11 has "torment ascends forever." Previous to Day 1, no matter what the sin, all have had the possibility of repenting of their sins and accepting Jesus as their Lord and Savior prior to a physical death and escaping an eternity in hades.

The consequence of Revelation 14:9–11 seems to be the *strong delusion* of 2 Thessalonians 2:11–12. This delusion prevents someone from knowing the truth while still alive on earth, and therefore repenting of their sin before they later physically die. So, on Day 1 forward it does not seem possible to witness to them.

What other options do we have to harmonize Scripture? Some may say taking the mark of the beast alone condemns someone to eternity in hades. If that were true, then consider it would mean you (and not God) could condemn any one by forcibly giving them the mark of the beast. That on the surface would go against the Scriptural free will of determining your own spiritual destiny in eternity. Revelation 14:9–11 says it requires more than just taking the mark of the beast.

> But the Spirit explicitly says that in later times some will fall away from the faith, paying attention to deceitful spirits and teachings of demons, by means of the hypocrisy of liars seared in their own conscience as with a branding iron. (1 Tim. 4:1–2 NASB)

> For this reason God (through the Holy Spirit) will send upon them a deluding influence so that they will believe what is false, in order that they all may be judged who did not believe the truth, but took pleasure in wickedness. (2 Thess. 2:11–12 NASB)

Index

abomination, xiii, 6, 9, 21–22, 36, 38, 39, 43, 47, 53, 55–56, 71
Armageddon, 74
chamber, 1, 14, 84–85, 87
Christmas, 31, 79
Days of Awe, x, 2, 8, 14, 40–41, 43, 59–74
Edgar Whisenant, 9–11, 18
Elijah, 3, 35–43
fury, 1, 82–89
grafted in, 51
Jehoshaphat battle, 2, 59, 64–74
Josephus, 50
Jubilee, 30
little while, 1, 82–85
Pontius Pilate, 31–32
Shekinah glory, 72

Scripture Index

Leviticus
- 23:4 7
- 25:9 30
- 26:33 50

Deuteronomy
- 24:5 73
- 30:5 53

2 Kings
- 2:11 3
- 20:1–11 27

Isaiah
- 24:1 46
- 26:20 84

Daniel
- 9:24 15
- 9:26 88
- 9:26–27 75
- 9:27 .... 6, 21, 55
- 11:39 88
- 12:11–12 47

Ezekiel
- 11:17 53
- 30:5–6 88
- 38:12 76
- 43:2 73

Hosea
- 6:1–2 .... 31, 79

Joel
- 2:31–32 .... 64, 66

Zechariah

12:8–10	15
14:4	67
14:4–5	57
14:6–8	57
14:8	56, 68, 76
14:10	57

Malachi

3:1–3	39
4:1	69
4:2–3	70
4:5	35

Matthew

12:32	90
13:38–39	61
15:24	51
17:12–13	38
24:1–2	10
24:2	50
24:9	5
24:15	6
24:16	56
24:19–20	55
24:21	5
24:22	25
24:27	73
24:29	5, 86
24:31	13
24:34	10
24:36	28
24:36–39	21
26:31	5
27:52–53	51

Luke
- 17:24 .... 3, 38, 72
- 17:29 3

John
- 10:22–23 45
- 14:19 83
- 16:16 83
- 19:16 31

Acts
- 1:3 83
- 1:12 56
- 2:1–4 8
- 5:14–16 51

Ephesians
- 3:6 51

1 Corinthians
- 14:33 2
- 15:51–52 14

1 Thessalonians
- 4:16–18 14
- 5:4–5 28

2 Thessalonians
- 2:1–2 35
- 2:11–12 90

1 Timothy
- 4:1–2 90

2 Peter
- 3:8 .... 31, 79

Revelation

1:15	73
6:8	88
6:9	6
6:11	84
6:12	80
8:5	3, 17, 40
8:7	3
9:15	66
9:20–21	87
11:2	63
11:2–3	39
11:11–12	39–40
11:13	40
11:19	38, 40, 72
12:6	15
12:13–14	15
12:14	72
14:9	90
14:12	88
14:14	64
14:15–16	64
14:17	64
14:18–19	64
14:20	64
17:16–17	89

Apocrypha Index

1 Maccabees
    4:59 47